# A Memoir of Injustice

By the Younger Brother of James Earl Ray,
Alleged Assassin of Martin Luther King, Jr.

## Jerry Ray

### As told to Tamara Carter

Afterword by Judge Joe Brown

A Memoir of Injustice: By the Younger Brother of James Earl Ray, Alleged Assassin of Martin Luther King, Jr.

Copyright © 2011 Jerry Ray; Tamara Carter. All Rights Reserved.
Presentation Copyright © 2011 Trine Day, LLC

Published by:
Trine Day LLC
PO Box 577
Walterville, OR 97489
1-800-556-2012
www.TrineDay.com
publisher@TrineDay.net

Library of Congress Control Number: 2010939684


Ray, Jerry,
A Memoir of Injustice: By the Younger Brother of James Earl Ray,
Alleged Assassin of Martin Luther King, Jr—1st ed.
p. cm.   (acid-free paper)
Includes references and index.
Epub (ISBN-13) 978-1-936296-61-3 (ISBN-10) 1-936296-61-6
Kindle (ISBN-13) 978-1-936296-62-0 (ISBN-10) 1-936296-62-4
Print (ISBN-13) 978-1-936296-05-7 (ISBN-10) 1-936296-05-5
1. King, Martin Luther, — Jr., — 1929-1968 — Assassination.
2. Ray, James Earl, — 1928-1998. 3. United States — Politics and
government — History. 4. United States — Corruption—History. 5.
Conspiracies — United States. I. Title

First Edition
10 9 8 7 6 5 4 3 2 1

Printed in the USA
Distribution to the Trade by:
Independent Publishers Group (IPG)
814 North Franklin Street
Chicago, Illinois 60610
312.337.0747

*Well, first, I didn't kill Dr. King.*

— James Earl Ray

*America will never have the benefit of Mr. Ray's trial, which would have produced new revelations about the assassination of Martin Luther King Jr. as well as establish the facts concerning Mr. Ray's innocence.*

— King family

*There is abundant evidence that there was a high level conspiracy in the assassination of my husband.*

— Coretta Scott King

*Injustice anywhere is a threat to justice everywhere.*

— Martin Luther King, Jr.

Dr. Martin Luther King, Jr. speaking at interfaith civil rights rally, San Francisco Cow Palace, June 30, 1964.

Photo courtesy of George Conklin.

# PUBLISHER'S FOREWORD

*This is my story, for what it's worth.*
*A little advice, you know it never hurt.*
*This world is so cruel, I hope you know what I mean.*
*You've got to keep on the move, nothing comes to a sleeper but a dream.*
— Lowell Fulsom

History stalks us constantly, coming from many directions, angles and attitudes. And as Henry L. Stimson said, "History is often not what actually happened but what is recorded as such." As a member of a secret society, the Order of Skull & Bones, Stimson knew. He served six presidents, occupying positions such as US Attorney, Governor-General of the Philippines, Secretary of State and Secretary of War (twice).

With *A Memoir of Injustice,* Jerry Ray and Tamara Carter expand our understanding of history, pointing away from the "recorded" version towards "what actually happened."

The official story of the murder of Martin Luther King, Jr. has been heartily debunked in books, and in court decisions. But even with the King family supporting his innocence, the vital facts of James Earl Ray's case have been strangely absent from mainstream exploration and discourse.

Not because we aren't curious, but by design. It is beneficial for some to let the discord of our ignorance and confusion fester.

Lawyer and author Dr. William Pepper bluntly told me in 2005 that he had an open invitation to appear on the NBC's *Today* show, as long as he *didn't* bring up his two thought-provoking books that expose the lies and fallacies found within the official version of the King assassination.

Given this reality, how can it be surprising that a February 2010 Zogby poll of likely voters declared that the news media is held in the least regard among American institutions, with only 21% of the population holding our fourth estate in "some" or a "lot" of confidence. The next lowest in esteem were labor unions, Wall Street, Big Banks and corporations. The poll results showed that twice as many trust the government as trust the news media. Yet, even with this amazing lack of public trust, the immense influence of our media continues.

Whatever the reasons behind the media's lack of candor, the effect is immensely deleterious to our republic, exasperating social anxieties, while cloaking corruption that decays our institutions, erodes our liberties and waylays our children.

*A Memoir of Injustice* gives us a sibling's view of, and insight into a national tragedy, and shows us the very real human consequences of being a brother to James Earl Ray. When caught in the cross hairs of history, destiny tugs in many directions, and many do not survive the onslaught of notoriety. Jerry Ray has felt the heat of the spotlight, but also has had the opportunity to reflect. He shares with us his good times, his bad times, his in-between times … and a fuller realization of what actually transpired in April 1968 in Memphis.

Today the propaganda is thick, whipped up to a frothy pitch, serving as a disconcerted backdrop to everyday life. Can "we the people" survive, in any rational form? What will our children do? How will they live? The future is what *we* create.

*Now is the time for all good men and women to come to the aid of their country.* This is not a class. This is not an exercise. This is life, the real deal. Will we stand-up and take back our country from the crooks, cronies and cabals? We do not need violence, do not need partisanship, secular or religious. Simply, our Founding Fathers' life, liberty and the pursuit of happiness.

Time will tell…

Onward to the Utmost of Futures!

Kris Millegan
Publisher
TrineDay
January 20, 2011

*We dedicate this book to*
*James Earl Ray*
*and*
*Reverend Dr. Martin Luther King, Jr.*

*~both innocent victims*

# ACKNOWLEDGMENTS

Jerry Ray:

I have so many people to acknowledge because so many individuals have helped me over the years. Thank you to Andrew Young, Harold Weisberg, Attorney Lewis Garrison, Mike Vinson and my family. Thanks to Lyndon Barsten, who did so much research and uncovered so much evidence, proving that Jimmy was innocent.

Thanks to Attorney Bill Pepper, who represented my brother Jimmy until the day he died. Also, thank you to my friend Dick Gregory, along with Mark Lane. Together you fought to get the truth out, and I appreciate your efforts.

I am forever grateful to the Martin Luther King family – Coretta Scott King, Dexter King and the rest of the family, for working all of these years to find out the truth. In addition, thank you for believing in, publicly proclaiming and supporting my brother's innocence.

A special thank you to Michael Gabriel, author of *James Earl Ray, The Last Days of Inmate #65477*, for moving from Baltimore to Nashville, visiting my brother in prison daily and taking him juice for a year when he got sick. You were a real big help to Jimmy. In addition, thank you for giving me permission to reveal the secret letters.

Thank you to Trine Day for publishing my story.

Several honest people want to know who really killed MLK, and they all fought with me to get my brother's rifle returned and tested. We are all sure that it was a throw-down gun, and so I want to thank them – T Carter, Attorney Barry Bachrach and Judge Joe Brown.

Tamara Carter:

*I am grateful to all who have crossed my path – whether you were a*
*help or a hindrance – because everything serves a purpose in the end.*
                                    — Joseph M. Marshall III, Sicangu Lakota

Genuine thanks to my publisher, Trine Day, especially Kris, for seeing the value of Jerry's story. Many thanks to my editor at Trine Day, Margot White. You are a brilliant woman with remarkable integrity.

I am forever grateful to Eliza Dolin of Ivy Quill Editing. E, you are the best representative this side of the Mississippi! Working with you brought me joy. A special thanks to Landmark Printing of Alexandria, Virginia for great work.

Extra special gratitude to Andy Winiarczyk – proprietor of The of Last Hurrah Bookshop, John Armstrong, Marty Bragg, Lyndon Barsten, and Phil Little Thunder for loyal friendship, wisdom and support. Mike Vinson, you are a genius at your craft! Thank you for your research assistance. Thanks to Lewis Garrison, Esq. for your legal expertise and assistance in our quest to reclaim and test the rifle. Michael Gabriel, thank you for offering Jimmy love and compassion during his final days. My sincere appreciation to Dr. Bill Pepper for support, encouragement and friendship.

John Judge, this book would not have been possible without you. Your intellect is unmatched, and I value your friendship beyond words.

Barry Bachrach, Esq., thank you so very, very much for handling the legal aspects of this book, serving as Jerry's attorney in his quest to reclaim and test the rifle and composing the foreword for this book – all pro bono. You are an extraordinary human being.

Judge Joe, thank you for sharing your knowledge – as only you can – and writing the afterword for this book. You are a generous genius. It is an honor and privilege to call you my friend.

Jerry, thank you for giving me this opportunity and for your unwavering trust. Most importantly, thank you for bringing joy and laughter into my life. You have taught me that humor has the power to save the day! Also, thank you to the Ray family.

Heartfelt thanks to my parents. I am grateful that you taught me that my struggles are far more significant than my successes. Thank you for helping me through both. Mom, I can never thank you enough for your patience and confidence. You are the best critical reader, research assistant and editor ever!

Thanks to the Creator for blessing me with numerous trials and tribulations in this life, for without them, I would lack character and strength, and I might not understand or appreciate the beauty of each sunrise – and the gift of a new day.

August 2010

# TABLE OF CONTENTS

Jerry Ray in 1957, while incarcerated at Jefferson City State Prison, Jefferson City, MO, the prison from which his brother James Earl Ray escaped in 1967.

Photo courtesy of Jerry Ray.

# FOREWORD

I was introduced to Jerry Ray by Tamara Carter towards the end of 2002. I knew Tamara through our mutual interest in justice and her work as a researcher and historian. Suffice it to say, Tamara was a great inspiration to both Jerry Ray and me as we tried to uncover evidence that would support the innocence of James Earl Ray.

I spoke to Jerry Ray occasionally over the telephone in late 2002 and early 2003 to discuss our mutual views on his brother's innocence and I first met him in April of 2003. Probably the highest compliment I can pay Jerry is to attest that he is a genuine and sincere human being. In a society where most people wear so many masks that they cannot remember which one they are wearing, it was refreshing to meet someone so consistently candid and unpretentious, regardless of the topic. We never seemed to run out of topics, or opinions, or stories for our conversations, and there was never any doubt where Jerry stood on every one of them.

Inevitably, our discussions turned to stories from Jerry's life, those involving his brother James Earl Ray, and Jerry's unwavering belief in his brother's innocence. Jerry's enthusiastic desire to prove his brother's innocence was infectious, and our discussions typically focused on his efforts to acquire the gun allegedly used by his brother to shoot Dr. Martin Luther King. Jerry was not seeking the gun as a collector's item, for posterity, but rather to conduct tests that could establish that his brother's gun was not the murder weapon.

During these discussions in 2002, I learned that Jerry, in his capacity as executor of the estate of James Earl Ray, had filed a pro se action against William Gibbons (District Attorney of Shelby County, Tennessee), William Key (Criminal Court Clerk of Shelby County, Tennessee), and the State of Tennessee. He was seeking a return of the rifle owned by his brother, James Earl Ray, that had been seized as evidence in his prosecution for the murder of Dr. Martin Luther King, Jr. Jerry explained that he had filed the action pro se because he could not find a lawyer in Tennessee who would represent him in this important suit to regain custody of the rifle.

Though not trained in the law, Jerry wrote a coherent and persuasive Complaint to the court, seeking return of the gun that had been used in the case against his brother. Since there were no pending criminal appeals or other litigation involving James Earl Ray for the alleged murder of Dr. King, Jerry Ray, as executor of his deceased brother's estate, demanded the return of the Remington Gamemaster Rifle to the estate. Defendants had refused to do so and, to the extent that Defendants claimed that the Remington Gamemaster Rifle was used in the commission of a crime, Jerry alleged that the State of Tennessee had failed to perform any reliable test that could establish that the Remington Gamemaster was used in the murder of Dr. King. In fact, in the complaint, Jerry pointed out that there has never been any decision by any court in the United States holding that the Remington Gamemaster Rifle was used in the commission of any crime, let alone the murder of Dr. King.

Jerry's lawsuit therefore squarely raised the issue of whether the Remington Gamemaster Rifle was used in the murder of Dr. King. Had the suit proceeded to trial, Jerry was prepared to have the gun tested to establish that it was not the murder weapon. However, the lawsuit died early because the State of Tennessee moved to dismiss the case, and, due to Jerry's lack of legal training, he did not realize that he had to file an appeal to the State's motion to dismiss his complaint or at least appear in Court to oppose it. So, Jerry waited for the Court to issue a decision, not realizing what those trained in the law knew – that the case would be dismissed. In fact, in May of 2002, the Tennessee court dismissed the case because of Jerry Ray's failure to appear in court and appeal the dismissal.

Jerry filed a timely appeal and while the appeal was pending, he discussed the case with me, including his frustration about not being able to find an attorney to assist him due to the sensitive subject matter of the case. Spurred by the emotional support of Tamara Carter who wholeheartedly supported Jerry's efforts to prove his brother's innocence, I eagerly offered to handle the appeal for Jerry. I knew it would be difficult to overturn the lower court decision even though Jerry's case had only been pending about three months before it was dismissed. Moreover, Tennessee courts generally regard dismissal as a harsh sanction that is not favored in circumstances where lesser sanctions are available, particularly when the case has just been filed.

In reality, however, this was not a case the Tennessee appellate courts would want to resuscitate once it had been killed. Allowing this case to proceed would very likely result in testing the gun – which would reveal that James Earl Ray did not kill Dr. King. Despite the odds, I knew that I could not let Jerry down or let his dream of proving his brother's innocence die.

Putting aside the procedural issue upon which the case had been erroneously dismissed, the State of Tennessee advanced three arguments for dismissing Jerry's case: 1) sovereign immunity; 2) that this issue was decided in the case of Hays v. Montague, 860 S.W. 2d 403 (Tenn. App. 1993); 3) and that the case was barred by the statute of limitations. In my opinion, none of the State's substantive arguments had merit. The reasons involve points of law related to jurisdiction and custody of evidence, specifically the gun allegedly used to kill Martin Luther King, Jr.

Therefore, we sought further appellate review of this decision by the Tennessee Supreme Court. We felt strong that the Tennessee Supreme Court should have taken the case and should have found that Jerry properly filed this case in the Circuit Court, which has jurisdiction over civil claims of violations of both the U.S. and Tennessee constitutions. On the basis of jurisdictional arguments, we asked the Supreme Court to remand the case to the trial court so that it could address the substantive issues raised by Mr. Ray's case, particularly those related to Ray's gun. Not surprisingly, the Tennessee Supreme Court denied further appellate review and allowed the proce dural dismissal to stand.

I have since continued to maintain contact with Jerry, but due to a change in my circumstances, I have not been able to assist him in his continuing crusade to have the truth be published about the murder of Dr. King. I am hopeful that the publication of this book brings with it a resurgence of interest in establishing the truth. While exonerating James Earl Ray will not reveal all the facts underlying the murder of Dr. King, it will be an important key to unlocking many aspects of the truth which have, to date, not been revealed to the public.

One of the simplest things that can be done – but which have been blocked up to now – is the definitive testing of the gun purportedly used by James Earl Ray. The gun is displayed in the National Civil Rights Museum, which is located where Dr. King was assassinated on April 4, 1968, pursuant to a an agreement with the State of Tennessee.

My hope is that this book will stir the interest of a new generation of researchers and/or lawyers to search for and find the truth. We owe it to Jerry to exonerate his brother and, just as important, we all owe it to this great country to expose the dirty secrets that certain people try to keep hidden. We cannot truly consider ourselves free if we allow the truth to be manipulated and permit our history to be written by those who stand for evil rather than good.

Barry Bachrach, Esq.
April 2009

"Jerry and T." Jerry Ray and Tamara Carter in Memphis, TN, 2003.
Photo courtesy of Marty Bragg.

# PREFACE

I met Jerry Ray in 1997 at a Reverend Dr. Martin Luther King, Jr. conference, hosted by the Coalition on Political Assassinations and held at the Comfort Inn Hotel in downtown Memphis, Tennessee, just a few blocks from Beale Street. The meeting started just as I took my seat near the front of the lecture room. A few minutes later, whispers rippled across the assemblage as a solitary man came through the door and quietly took a seat. The message was passed around – the man who had just walked in was indeed Jerry Ray, the younger brother of James Earl Ray, alleged assassin of Martin Luther King, Jr.

Immediately following the speaker, Jerry slipped out of the room and stepped into an elevator. Not fast enough to catch the same elevator, I decided to race down the stairs in hopes of arriving at the ground floor before Jerry. Luckily, I succeeded – because, you see, as an historian and researcher, I had a burning desire to hear his side of the story. As Jerry stepped out of the elevator, I hurried over and introduced myself. After a slight – and understandable – hesitation on Jerry's part, we sat down and talked at length about his brother Jimmy (James Earl Ray) and the murder of Martin Luther King.

Over the years since then, Jerry and I developed a close friendship. We met often at Rendezvous, a world famous rib joint in Memphis, and the Cellar, a Nashville bar with a vast selection of imported beers. Although our visits included discussion of Jimmy and MLK, and Jerry's stories about his life, our main reason for getting together was to socialize. We simply enjoyed eating catfish or BBQ, washing it down with a Bass beer and sharing a few laughs.

I always told Jerry that our friendship came first; therefore, I did not wish to write about his family. I made this crystal clear over the years. Then, in 2008, Jerry asked me to write a book about his life. Initially, I declined his offer. However, after several persuasive conversations with Jerry, I realized that I needed to write this book for him. I believe that Jerry's story – the story that I wanted to hear when I first met him – is of significant value to all readers, for it serves as a counter-narrative to the official story and therefore provides a vital addition to the historical record.

This book is the result of many hours of discussion, personal interviews, telephone conversations and cassette-taped sessions with Jerry. Although researching and writing presented many challenges, Jerry made my task easier by evidencing a precise memory: he recounted virtually all of his life experiences exactly the same every time. An excellent storyteller and historian's dream, Jerry never embellished or altered his narrative, even slightly. The old saying holds true – the truth never changes. Jerry possesses a prodigious capacity for details, for accurate retention and recall of dates, times, places and names. His skills made it far easier to achieve my objective of telling Jerry's story in his voice, and not mine.

In addition to collecting Jerry's memories, I conducted exhaustive research on the Martin Luther King murder case and on James Earl Ray. By thoroughly examining both primary and secondary materials, I was able to verify Jerry's account, assure accuracy and put this narrative into historical context. I drew heavily on primary documents, including Freedom of Information Act releases, Federal Bureau of Investigation files, military records, trial transcripts, lawsuit depositions and interrogatories, United States Congressional publications, and United States Department of Justice archives. Newspaper stories, magazine and journal articles, relevant books and online publications provided additional source material.

Jerry Ray's purpose is not to solicit sympathy or pity for himself. In fact, he insists that he has experienced minimal suffering as a result of being the brother of James Earl Ray, in contrast to what Jimmy himself endured. Instead, through this narrative, Jerry wants to expose the reader to his truth – his brother's innocence and the continued injustice surrounding him. Yes, the injustice still persists to this day. The Tennessee courts repeatedly rule against retesting the rifle that James Earl Ray purchased, even though they have an unsolved murder case in their files – and not just any murder, but the slaying of arguably the greatest civil rights leader of our time, Martin Luther King, Jr.

Most importantly, Jerry was the person closest to James Earl Ray. They shared secrets not known by anyone else. For the first time, Jerry Ray shares these confidences with the public, filling in many important pieces of the puzzle. It is all here – an impoverished childhood, break-ins, bank robberies, stabbings, shootings, a snitch, encrypted letters, escape plans, shadowy government figures, loud-mouthed lawyers, a dead judge, brothers in arms and the bond of love between brothers. Jerry's account is not a sugarcoated tale, but a raw and riveting memoir of injustice.

T Carter
February 2009

# A Memoir
# of Injustice

James Earl Ray at Brushy Mountain Prison in 1988.
Photo courtesy of Jerry Ray.

# CHAPTER ONE

# DIRT POOR – BUT NOT TRASH

P eople have been after me to do this book for more than thirty years now, and they often ask, "Jerry, why did you wait so long?" Well, I have been attempting to write my story since 1997. However, I experienced various obstacles along the way, including expired contracts, corrupt/suspicious writers, loss of interest in the book and changes in plans, etc. In 2008, I turned to Tamara Carter. The reason I wanted her to write my book is that she is very familiar with the case of my brother Jimmy [James Earl Ray]. There are very few people that I can count on and that I trust; Tamara is one of them.

I'm not asking for personal sympathy, or for you to like my brother Jimmy. I simply want to tell my story in order to expose the injustice and set the record straight. I ask only that you assess the information for yourself and draw your own conclusions. With that said, I'll begin where it all started.

*** 

In the early 1920s, my dad, George E. Ray, was convicted of burglary and sentenced to two to ten years. He was incarcerated at Iowa State Prison in Fort Madison, Iowa. It wasn't like it is now – with prisoners claiming guard brutality and civil liberties groups investigating charges of misconduct.

No-no, back then it was hard time. They would tie you up and work you over if you were guilty of any kind of infraction of the rules – and sometimes just for the plain ol' hell of it. After about two years, Dad made parole. Since he was from Keokuk, Iowa, that's where he was paroled. However, Dad was intent on making sure he didn't go back to that hellhole of a prison, so he left the State of Iowa, which automatically violated his parole. To the best of my knowledge, my dad never again returned to Iowa.

Shortly afterwards, around 1926, Dad met my mom, Lucille Maher, in Alton, Illinois. I'm not sure exactly why he went to Alton; I just know that's where he met my mother. Anyway, they got married soon after they met, took a short honeymoon to Florida, and returned to Alton to set up house. On March 10, 1928, Mom and Dad had their first child, a boy they named James Earl, the eldest of nine. He was named after my paternal grandfather, James Ray, and my uncle, Earl Ray, my dad's younger brother. Little did my parents know what the future had in store for little James Earl. My family called my brother Jimmy, not James Earl. The media used his full given name while reporting on the King assassination and they continue to do so. But to me, he was not James Earl Ray; he was my brother – Jimmy. After Jimmy came eight more children.

We moved around often back then. Our first move took us from Alton to Quincy, Illinois. The move was the result of my Dad making a shady deal with a local corn farmer. They were supposed to split the profits fifty/fifty, but my dad took the whole thing. The farmer called the sheriff to arrest my old man. When the sheriff arrived and attempted to arrest my dad, Mom told the sheriff that Dad was Uncle Earl, and that George Ray was not home. The sheriff believed her. Being a parole violator – something the local police didn't know about yet – and in trouble again, Dad figured it was best for the family to leave Alton. So, we moved to Quincy, Illinois where my grandparents, James and Lillian Ray, lived.

I was the fourth born child, coming into this world on July 16, 1935 in Quincy, Illinois. When I was about three months old, the family moved to Ewing, Missouri, about twenty miles from Quincy. We lived there from 1935 to 1944, and then moved again. In a period of only about two and a half years, we moved from Ewing to Quincy, to Galesburg [Illinois], to Hamil [Illinois], to Adams [Illinois], and back to Quincy. My dad being a parole violator and a fugitive on the run forced our family to be on the move constantly. The insecurities resulting from that unstable lifestyle no doubt contributed to us boys later getting involved in a life of crime.

In fact, my dad not only moved us frequently, but changed his last name, as well. First he changed it from Ray to Raynes (sometimes spelled Rayns), and later to Ryan. When they were ducking the authorities, my brothers Jimmy and John used Rayns quite a bit as an alias. In fact, the oldest four kids were born under the name Ray, the next three under Raynes, and the last two under Ryan. My dad was always changing his last name to evade authorities – so they wouldn't locate him. He had the letters JR tattooed on his arm, so he always selected aliases with those initials. In those days, if you wanted to change your identity, you could move to a different location and use almost any name you wanted to – as long as you didn't get into trouble and draw unnecessary attention to yourself. You couldn't do that now, though. If you apply for any form of identification or credit or open a bank account these days, they want to know everything about you.

A few years after we moved to Ewing, my sister Margie, about six years old at the time, was playing with matches and caught her dress on fire. Mom jumped on her and tried to put out the fire, but Margie was burned badly. They rushed her to the hospital in Quincy but, unfortunately, she died a few days later.

The other big tragedy for our family in those years involved my younger brother Frank who was killed in a car wreck in 1963 at the age of 19. What I remember most about Frank was that his favorite signer was Roy Orbison, and I liked Orbison too. That's about the time I started listening to country music instead of rock: Ray Price, Webb Pierce – singers like that.

Growing up in Missouri, we raised almost everything we ate and drank: dairy cows, chickens, tomatoes, and potatoes. My dad got a job with the Works Progress Administration, known as the WPA, for short. The WPA, created by President Franklin Delano Roosevelt (FDR) as a part of his New Deal program, provided jobs and income to the unemployed during the Great Depression in the United States. My dad brought home only a few dollars, however, and we barely got by. But, it wasn't only my family. Almost all families back then had it rough. After all, my early years in Ewing, Missouri were right after the Depression. I've read where my family once lived in a house with a dirt floor. I can't say for sure that I remember us living in a house with a dirt floor, but neither am I going to deny the possibility.

Our life in Missouri was simple, poor, and ordinary for a small town in America. One other aspect of it is crucial to mention, however: it was totally white.

Although I now know that the Ku Klux Klan [KKK] was rampant throughout America during the 1930s and 1940s, I don't remember even once seeing or hearing about them during my childhood years, much less having been influenced by them. After the assassination of Martin Luther King, Jr. in Memphis, April 4, 1968, a lot of puppet writers for the government, including George McMillan, a writer in the service of official government agencies. I had a lot of contact with him over the years and I became deeply familiar with his distortions and outright fabrications. He tried to portray my family as a bunch of whiskey-guzzling, cross-burning racists who hated everybody who wasn't white – blacks, Jews, Latinos, anybody. Although these bogus allegations had no basis in fact, they were hatched by certain writers to convince the gullible public that Jimmy (James Earl Ray, as they called him) had been raised in a bigoted environment, had evolved into a racist because of it, and had killed King because of those racist views.

During the first nine years of my life while living in Ewing, Missouri, I never saw a single black person – not one. In Ewing, all the kids in school were white; all the stores in town were run by white people; and the only people patronizing the stores were whites. The only time I or anybody in my family ever saw a black person during those early years was when we would go to Quincy, about twenty miles away, to visit my grandparents, which was very seldom. As I've said over the years since the King assassination, how could we have hatred for a group of people we never were around? If my family harbored any racist sentiments, prejudice or hatred when I was growing up, it would had to have been against whites because they were the only people we had any personal contact with back then. And, on top of that, my mother's favorite athlete was Joe Louis – black – and Jimmy's favorite athlete was Hank Greenberg – Jewish.

I started my schooling in Ewing, Missouri and ended it at the Sheridan Reformatory in Sheridan, Illinois. You could get a high school diploma at a reformatory, but I never did get my high school diploma. I made it through elementary school and finished one year of high school. I'm pretty sure that Jimmy finished the tenth grade. I know that Susan finished high school, and maybe Carol did too. I'm not that certain about the education level of the rest of my brothers and sisters.

Looking back on my early years in Ewing, I recall that Jimmy and I were extra close. One of my strongest memories is that he, seven years older than I was, did a lot of things that most big brothers do for their little brothers. The thing about Jimmy, though, was that he never would show you his true feelings, his emotions. For example, he would come home with a candy bar and not offer me any at first. After just a little while, though, he would pull me off to the side and tell me that he didn't want the candy bar – hadn't even broken the wrapper – so he was going to let me have it. Even as a young kid,

I knew that he'd purposely bought the candy for me, but he didn't want me to know that he had. I now realize that was his way of keeping an edge.

*** 

Over the years, many people – writers, reporters and the merely curious – have asked me what caused Jimmy, John and me to become involved in a life of crime. No doubt, living in virtual poverty, always on the move, and having to lie about your true name had its effect on us growing up. More than that, though, I feel that what caused us to choose the wrong side of the law back then were the people we hung around with. For example, in addition to our dad having served time in prison, my Uncle Earl was a hardcore criminal – a true badass – and he, no doubt, had an effect on us because we all looked up to him. He taught us boys not to take any shit from anybody, no matter how big or how bad, even if it meant getting your eyes stomped out of your head. Our parents did not encourage us, as kids, towards violence, especially starting it. We were only to fight when protecting ourselves. We were like a normal family back then. When I was in jail, I learned if you didn't fight back, you would be killed.

In addition, Quincy, Illinois was wide open and rather lawless when I was growing up – gambling, whorehouses, bootleg joints – every damn thing! It served as the perfect breeding ground for crime, and this environment seemed 'natural' to Jimmy and John and me because we grew up in it.

Cairo and Quincy, Illinois were often written about in magazines because of their reputation for rampant crime. Jimmy told me about going into those rough joints in Quincy with his namesake, Uncle Earl, who wasn't all that big, but he was wiry and had those steel-piercing eyes. As soon as he walked into a joint, it would get quiet as a mouse. Anybody with any sense knew that if he messed with Uncle Earl the wrong way, there would be a heavy price to pay. One of Jimmy's first ventures over to the wrong side of the law occurred when he tagged along with Uncle Earl to one of the whorehouses in Quincy and ended up running an errand for the madam of that place. Jimmy even mentions this in his book (*Who Killed Martin Luther King? The True Story By the Alleged Assassin*) because it made such a lasting impression on him.

In March 1946, Jimmy enlisted in the U.S. Army. Although I was only about eleven years old, I still remember it just as if it was yesterday because I missed him so much, and as close as we were. Jimmy did his basic training at a signal corps base near Joplin, Missouri and four months later, he was stationed in Bamberg, Germany, near Nuremberg.

I have a picture of Jimmy when he was home on leave from the Army. I am standing beside him and he is playfully pulling on my ear. In 1948 my brother Jimmy was discharged from the Army and returned to Quincy. I later found out that he had gotten into trouble for missing guard duty and had done time in the stockade. That incident had led to his discharge, which was neither an honorable, nor a dishonorable one – somewhere in between. Friends, family, everyone who knew Jimmy was surprised that he had been discharged from the military under those conditions. We all thought that if anybody in our family would amount to something, it would be Jimmy because he was so bright. Also, Jimmy wasn't a bad-looking guy. Women noticed him. Jimmy always took good care of himself by exercising and watching what he ate. He lectured me to stop smoking and soaking the suds.

After Jimmy was discharged from the Army, he returned home to Quincy for a while. There wasn't much going on there, however, and he was restless. As a result, he left Quincy and hoboed his way out to Los Angeles, California.

Los Angeles was where Jimmy first got into trouble with the authorities. As he later told me, about the only work he could find was day-to-day, jobs that were usually for migrant workers. Almost starving to death, Jimmy broke into a business office in Los Angeles and stole some office equipment. A day or two later, he was identified and arrested. Jimmy was ultimately convicted for that break-in and he served about four months in prison, from around December 1949 until March 1950.

However, none of the family saw Jimmy until around May of 1950 because he had to hobo his way back to Quincy from Los Angeles and it took him awhile. Hopping the trains was illegal back then. In fact, while Jimmy was on the rails from Los Angeles, he was arrested in Cedar Rapids, Iowa. As the train passed through Cedar Rapids, it made a stop and a deputy sheriff, specifically looking for hobos, spotted Jimmy and arrested him for having a suspicious roll of coins on him. Sure enough, Jimmy had broken into a restaurant and stolen the coins before he left Los Angeles. The authorities in Cedar Rapids, however, never could gather enough evidence to convict him. So, after about a month of detention, they had to release him. Being locked up in Cedar Rapids for a month lengthened the time it took Jimmy to get home.

***

Leroy Houston, Jim Baker and I were neighbors in Quincy and we were about the same age. The three of us lived just off Third Street and in those days, it was lined with taverns, gambling joints and whorehouses. We started committing strong-arm robberies together in the late forties. We were game for anything and everything, just poor boys trying to make some fast bucks here and there, any way we could. We'd catch a drunk coming out of one of those places, and if we thought we could physically handle him, we'd strong-arm him. We'd run up on him, grab him, drag him over to a side alley, knock him to the ground and take everything he had – money, watches, rings, whatever. If he was some big, rough-looking badass, though, we'd leave him alone, because we were fairly young and not yet all that big ourselves.

One of those robberies that I remember vividly was the one that Leroy and I did together, just the two of us. It happened at a place called the Cozy Inn, only about a block and a half from my house. The Cozy Inn had a small bar that held maybe about twelve to fifteen people. All the prostitutes would hang out at the bar. A "John" would walk in, have a drink with a prostitute of his choice, cut a deal with her, and take her back to one of the rooms right behind the bar and have sex with her. On this particular night it was cold as hell and I was wearing a pair of black gloves to keep my hands from freezing. Leroy and I snuck around to the outside window of the room where one of the 'Johns' and one of the prostitutes were getting it on. You could hear them grunting, breathing hard and the bedsprings creaking. The Venetian blinds on the window of their room were open enough to allow you to peak inside the room, so Leroy and I looked. The man and the prostitute were too busy to notice. We happened to see the man's pants hanging on the back of a chair, just a foot or so from the window. I had an idea….

I gave Leroy one of my gloves. He put it on his right hand, and I kept the other one on my left hand. Leroy then let fly with his gloved hand and knocked out the glass window. As soon as he rammed his hand through the window, I reached through it, grabbed the man's pants, and we hauled ass to a park about three blocks away. His wallet had about fourteen or fifteen dollars in it, which today would be like a hundred dollars. Sex with a prostitute cost about three to five dollars back then, and what we got probably was the change left over from a twenty. As we went through the John's wallet, we found his driver's license and discovered that he happened to be a farmer from Missouri. After we took the money, we threw his pants, wallet, car keys and driver's license down a sewer drain in the park. Leroy and I laughed all the way home because we figured the guy was married, and he was going to have a hard time explaining to his wife where his wallet was – not to mention his pants – and why he didn't come home in the same clothes he'd left in.

This petty theft of the John by Leroy and me is just one example of how wild and reckless it was in Quincy during the time frame we're talking about. But there were other elements that show this as well. For example, during the 1950s, there was an Illinois state senator known as Senator Dick, or 'Dick', for short. He was a big, stout, tough-looking guy. Dick was his last name, but that wasn't the only reason he was called Senator Dick. He would cruise downtown Quincy almost every night in his Chrysler Imperial, looking for teenage boys. He would pick up some young boy, take him to his house, and pay the boy to let Senator Dick perform oral sex on him. When Senator Dick had finished and had paid him, the fine legislator would beat the poor kid horribly. I'm not talking about just slapping these kids around, but thoroughly battering and beating them. Senator Dick, though messed up in the head, had a reputation for being one tough son-of-a-bitch. His trademark saying – "there is nothing I like better than sucking dicks and whooping ass!" – turned out to be true.

In March 1950, when I was almost fifteen years old, I was arrested and convicted for one of the strong-arm robberies that I'd committed with Leroy and Jim in Quincy. I don't actually remember the specifics because it was just like many such robberies, except that we got caught. Actually, Leroy, Jim and I were already on probation for a prior strong-arm. Consequently, I was sentenced to the St. Charles Training School in St. Charles, Illinois.

The St. Charles facility was in between a regular school and a reformatory. Right after I arrived, I had my first two – and only – actual fights with blacks. The first one involved a black kid about my age who was bullying the other boys. Even though he was smaller than I was – I wasn't very big at that age – he was a tough kid and knew how to fight. As soon as I arrived at St. Charles, he made a beeline for me and got in my face, telling me how bad he was and what he was going to do to me. I never said a word. I just hauled off and busted his nose. Blood spurted everywhere. After that, he never messed with me again.

The second black kid I fought at St. Charles was bigger than I was, but about the same age. I can't remember for sure what the fight was about, but I think it had something to do with the chow line. Anyway, we'd been arguing with each other for some time, so the school officials put boxing gloves on us and let us get inside the ring to duke it out. That second black kid got the best of me this time. So I've had two fights with blacks – won one and lost one.

\*\*\*

I was paroled in March 1951. I was out for only three weeks when I burglarized a place, violating my parole. I was sent back to St. Charles. Yes, I was paroled and sent back, all within one month.

Not too long after they sent me back to St. Charles, I took part in a hellacious riot. We tore that place to pieces – broke dishes, windows, everything. I guess the reason we rioted was the same reason we were in there: to rebel against a structured society that adopted, adhered to, and enforced rules and laws. The riot was so violent and got so out of control that the guards couldn't stop us, and they ended up calling the state highway patrol. Several guards and prisoners were hurt badly. For my involvement in the riot at St. Charles, I was sentenced to one and one-half years at the Sheridan Reformatory, a much rougher place. I graduated from Sheridan Reformatory in January 1953, never once getting out until that release.

Just before my release from Sheridan, in May 1952, Jimmy had been convicted of robbing a Chicago cab driver and had been sentenced to a couple of years at the medium security prison in Pontiac, Illinois. He was released in the spring of 1954. This particular incident illustrates how my family has been misrepresented by the mainstream media.

In the spring of 1998, author and attorney Gerald Posner – whom I sometimes called 'Posie Wosie' – published a book called *Killing the Dream* – his version of the King assassination.

Of course, Posner said that James Earl Ray killed King because Posner is a government writer and he had to write what his paymasters told him to write. In his book, Posner states that in May 1952, while I was working at a riding stable in Le Grange, Illinois, a suburb of Chicago, I read in the newspaper about Jimmy robbing the cab driver and that I sent a clipping of the story to our mother.[1]

Posner's statement that I was working at a riding stable in Le Grange in 1952 is utter fabrication – I was locked up during all of 1952. My official legal records prove that because of my role in the St. Charles riots, I remained, at Sheridan Reformatory, without parole, from March 1951 until January 1953. I confronted Posner with his factual error when he was doing a book signing in Memphis, Tennessee in April 1998. It was the 30-year anniversary of the King assassination. The audience started siding with me, and we almost had a riot – right there at Posner's book signing.

Posner's response was to shut down his book signing. He was smart to do it because had he kept it open, I would have exposed his book for what was – "literary Swiss Cheese, more holes than substance," as one writer put it. Because Posner is a lawyer, he knows how to dodge a question, but he can't deny what happened at the book signing because the whole thing is captured on video. You would think Posner would have gone to the trouble of checking my records before writing incorrect information. However, if your primary objective is money and not getting at the truth, researching facts is irrelevant.

\*\*\*

In 1952, my dad left my mother for a woman named Ruby Carpenter. Dad and Ruby worked together at the Hotel Lincoln-Douglas in Quincy and they took off for St. Louis together. Although Mom and Dad never got back together again, it was several years before they actually divorced. After Dad and Mom's divorce became final, Dad and Ruby married.

1        Gerald Posner, *Killing the Dream* (New York: Random House, 1998), 105.

Several factors contributed to my dad leaving my mom: Mom had a drinking problem; Jimmy, John and I were always in and out of trouble and doing time; Dad was working himself to the bone and not getting anywhere; and Ruby offered Dad a break from his burdens. I'm not siding with Dad for leaving Mom – he shouldn't have! I'm just addressing the reality of a sad situation.

Maxie, the youngest child, was only a few months old when Dad took off. Since we had barely been able to get by as it was, Dad leaving our family brought on even greater hardships. By the time I was released from Sheridan in January 1953, our family situation had become unbearable, with several young children to support and no conceivable way to provide for them.

Not too long after this, the state removed Melba, Frank, Susan, and Maxie from our house and placed them in foster homes around Quincy. For some reason, the state didn't take Carol. Instead, she went to St. Louis to live with Dad and his new wife Ruby. Maxie was adopted out. I haven't seen him since sometime in 1953 when he was about one year old. I wouldn't know him if I met him walking down the street. Social Services eventually placed Melba in a state home and she continues to live there to this day. On the one hand, the breakup of our family was sad. On the other hand, it was a blessing in disguise, considering everything that has happened since then.

When Dad left, Mom's drinking got worse. However, she was not completely nonfunctioning. Even though she was drinking heavily, she still managed to hold down a job. About a year after Dad left, however, she got so sick that she couldn't work. In 1953, she went to the local hospital and the doctors removed part of her liver. I was with her at the hospital when the doctor told her that if she stopped drinking her liver would grow back and she could live a fairly normal, healthy life, possibly to an old age because Mom naturally was a strong woman. And my mom did quit drinking ... for a while. She went back to work and continued working after her liver scare.

After I was released from Sheridan in 1953, my brother John and I stole a car and robbed a combination store/tavern in Adams, Illinois, just a few miles from Quincy. We loaded down the car with all the cigarettes and liquor it could hold and headed back to Quincy. In those days, you could easily get rid of all of the cigarettes and whiskey you could get your hands on. We planned to sell the cigarettes and liquor to a man named "Slats" Williams, a well-known local bootlegger/pimp who ran a combination tavern/whorehouse down on Third Street. When we got back to Quincy, John dropped me off at 214 Spring Street, where John and I lived with Mom. We stashed the liquor and cigarettes inside Mom's house and then John raced to the local park to dispose of the stolen car – the same park where Leroy Houston and I had thrown the farmer's emptied wallet and pants down the sewer drain a few years earlier.

While John was in the process of setting the stolen car on fire, the local police noticed the smoke and immediately arrived on the scene. They arrested John for car theft and, after searching the car and finding things they later connected to the robbery, they eventually charged him with burglary. John spent about seven years at Menard Prison for what we had done. Eventually, the local police figured out I was involved and they interrogated me heavily about it. But I kept my mouth shut and they never could make anything stick. And, of course, John wouldn't give up anything.

*** 

Members of my family served time in prison quite frequently during those years. Prior to his arrest for car theft, John had already served time for previous car theft and burglary in 1949. I remember visiting him while he was locked up inside the Quincy Jail, before he was sent up to Menard Prison. He told me he wanted to attempt an escape and asked me to sneak in some hacksaw blades. We had already talked about how we were going to pull it off. When you went to visit a prisoner, you had to check in at the front desk and show the guards anything and everything you planned to give to the prisoner you were visiting. However, on this particular day, I didn't declare anything. Instead, I hid some hacksaw blades inside some girlie magazines – the kind the guards wouldn't allow prisoners to have – and placed everything inside my shirt. They didn't have metal detectors back then, so I was able to sneak the hacksaw blades inside simply by hiding them in the magazines.

John already had some girlie magazines inside his cell that I had snuck in to him on a previous visit. So, when I reached John's cell and while we were talking, I slipped the girlie magazines to him under the door, with the hacksaw blades inside. John immediately slid his other girlie magazines out to me. A guard noticed the commotion and came over to me, standing at John's cell door with these girlie magazines in my hand. The guard asked me what I was doing with the girlie magazines. I told him that John had refused them. The guard then told me that John was smart for refusing that kind of magazine, but that I had to leave for attempting to sneak them to him. I left. While the guard had been occupied with me outside John's cell, John was able to stash the saw blades without drawing attention.

The next day, John sawed his way through the bars across the window at the rear of his jail cell. At that time, the Quincy Jail was only about a year old, and it was supposed to have been built with a strong enough gauge of steel that a prisoner couldn't saw out and escape. John proved that wrong – and he also proved that the contractor who built the Quincy Jail hadn't built it to specifications and had put one over on the state. While John was sawing his way out, one of the prisoners – a rat! – alerted the guards. When you're pulling a crime, it's the rats/snitches that you have to worry about, not the authorities. Since John's cell was on the third floor, he'd tied together some sheets with which to let himself down. As he was lowering himself down the wall, he looked down and there were the guards standing on the ground below with their guns trained on him. They told him to "come on down." Needless to say, John did not escape and they punished him for attempting.

As soon as John was caught attempting to escape, the police came to my place of work and said they knew what had happened, that I had slipped the blades to John inside the girlie magazines, and all of that had been a diversion to keep them sidetracked. I asked, "If you knew, then why didn't you arrest me?" They said they didn't know when it actually happened, but that they knew now. Of course, being the wise guy I was, I responded with, "If you didn't know at the scene, you don't know now. Look, I don't have any saw blades on me, and that's that." One cop looked at me as though he could kill me, hissing like a snake, but he and the others left. I never was charged with aiding John in that escape.

However, in February 1954, another friend, Mickey Walker, and I were convicted of burglary and sentenced to two years at Menard Prison in Illinois. John was already doing time at Menard, having been there since 1953 for the car theft and burglary. Also, Uncle Earl was doing time there when I arrived in 1954. I can't remember exactly why he was doing time, but I believe it was for murder or some kind of serious assault.

When I first arrived at Menard, I was constantly getting into trouble, smarting off to the guards, getting into fights, dumb shit. My punishment for those infractions was assignment to Gang #7, which was the coal pile detail. Along with the rest of Gang #7, I shoveled coal about eight hours a day. At the same time, Uncle Earl had made trustee and was a runner for the prison chaplain, a Catholic priest. A trustee in the prison is a convict that has earned a special security level. There are always a bunch of trustees in prison, working for different prison employees. They are like a foreman. It takes a while to become a trustee. You have to have a good record – not do anything bad for a while. They have many privileges and get special favors. Trustees work at their jobs completely on their own – virtually unsupervised. Uncle Earl worked for the Catholic Priest – he was the Priest's trustee. Another name for trustee was 'honor people.' A runner just means that the trustee runs errands.

When Uncle Earl would see me on the coal pile, he would tell the guard that the priest wanted to see me for some spiritual counseling. Earl would take me into the chaplain's quarters, where I would spend most of the day just kicked back and taking it easy. Sometimes the priest was there; sometimes he wasn't. It really didn't matter, either way, because Uncle Earl was in good with the priest, so the priest would go along with whatever. That's just the kind of guy Uncle Earl was – smooth and hard-edged. He had an overpowering effect on people.

\*\*\*

Jimmy was released from Pontiac Prison in the spring of 1954, having served a couple of years for robbing the cab driver in 1952. He came back to Quincy and became involved with Walter Rife, who had a brother named Lonnie Rife. Walter and Lonnie were local tough guys and hustlers – you couldn't trust either one of them. Uncle Earl, after being released from Menard, warned Jimmy about Walter Rife, but Jimmy didn't heed Uncle Earl's warning, and, before you knew it, sometime in 1955, not too long after being released from Pontiac, Jimmy was in trouble again. Jimmy later told me what happened.

Rife was originally from Kellerville, Illinois where he had just broken into the Kellerville Post Office and stolen all the money orders along with the official stamp that was used to validate money orders. Rife told Jimmy that if he would drive him to Florida, where Rife could forge and cash the money orders, then he would pay my brother for his troubles. Jimmy was in dire need of money, especially bond money to keep out of jail on some other burglary charges, so he agreed to drive Rife to Jacksonville, Florida. According to my brother, Rife cashed some of the stolen money orders along the way. Jimmy told me that he and Rife traveled in and out of several states cash-ing those money orders before they finally reached Hannibal, Missouri. For his part in that crime – a federal crime, since it involved money orders and crossing state lines – Jimmy was sentenced to three years and nine months, which he served from 1955 to 1958 at the federal penitentiary in Leavenworth, Kansas. Jimmy always thought that Rife, who had a lengthy criminal record, including several forgery convictions, had dropped a dime on him, since Rife received a lighter sentence – only three years.

Shortly after I was released on parole from Menard in November 1955, I went to work at the Hotel Lincoln-Douglas in Quincy. After I got off work one day, a crooked local cop, Burt Welde, pulled me over and took me into a side alley where he threw me up against the wall and told me he knew all about me and my brothers. If I didn't watch out, he said, he'd put me behind bars for good. Of course, given all the trouble I'd been in, my name was quite familiar to the local police. Uncle Earl once said that I must have had a vested interest in the Quincy newspaper, given how often my name had been printed in the court docket section. Anyway, after he finished telling me that he planned to lock me up for good, Burt Welde punched me in the eye. Not only did he bust open my eye, but his ring scraped my eyeball, and I almost went blind in that eye. I always wanted to get Welde back for hurting me for no reason, but I never did.

Around this same time, I started hanging out with a guy named Jack "Catman" Gawron. He and my mother had become friends after Mom and Dad split in 1952. Catman talked a tough game, but it turned out, he wasn't anything but an old wino who liked to brag. Some people will try to say that he was given the nickname Catman because he was some sort of high-tech cat burglar – not so! The actual reason he was called Catman is because he lived in this rundown, filthy apartment with about thirty or forty cats. I made the mistake of pulling off one job with Catman.

In early 1956, Catman, my cousin Charlie Cain, and I robbed a service station just across the bridge in Taylor, Missouri, the first small town you come to when you cross over from Quincy into Missouri. When we walked into the service station that night, each of us had on a full-face stocking mask. Charlie and I were packing pistols and Catman was carrying a double barrel, sawed-off shotgun. Catman Gawron, with all his tough talk, wouldn't even bring his shotgun up and point it at the service station attendant. He just held it down at his side the whole time. I got pissed off, pushed Catman to the side, and stuck my pistol in the attendant's face while Charlie cleaned out the cash register. I can't remember exactly how much loot we got, but it was several dollars. After Charlie finished cleaning out the register, we got out of there. I was so pissed at Catman that I considered pistol-whipping his chicken-shit ass on the way back to Quincy. However, I knew we needed to get out of Taylor, Missouri fast, so I managed to keep my cool. In time, I would have my day with Catman Gawron.

We were driving my car on that job – a Town & Country, with the wooden trim on the sides, easy to identify – and that's how the police ended up connecting me to the robbery and they arrested me. Initially, I was picked up by the Quincy police and locked up inside the Quincy jail. The Quincy police kept trying to get me to sign extradition papers to Missouri, but I kept refusing. At first, my probation officer told me not to sign any extradition papers. However, after the investigators talked to him, my probation officer told me that if I didn't sign the extradition papers he would revoke my probation and I would go to jail for a long time. Fearful of my probation officer's threats, I eventually signed the extradition papers and was taken to and locked up inside the jail in Monticello, Missouri. Monticello was the county seat for Taylor, where we'd robbed the service station. After I was locked up inside the Monticello Jail, the Missouri investigators told me they wanted Charlie Cain, not me. If I would rat out Charlie, they would cut me a good deal. Charlie had been in a bunch of trouble. The investigators and prosecutors probably would have taken it easier on me had I snitched, but I wasn't about to let them turn me into a rat, so I told them to go get screwed, which was stupid. Even though they did charge me, they never did take me to trial.

They kept me locked up in the Monticello Jail for several weeks, trying to get me to admit to robbing the service station and to rat on my cousin, Charlie. One time, the investigators tried to be slick. They said if I didn't do it, then for me to write down on a piece of paper the names of ten people I thought may have been involved. They were trying to trick me, as though I was some sort of an idiot. Well, that thoroughly pissed me off. I did write down ten names – totally bogus ones, only to confuse the investigators.

We finally got caught in Sikeston, Missouri, near the Arkansas border, about three hundred miles from Kirksville. The authorities flew us back to Kirksville in a Piper Club airplane. When I arrived at the Kirksville jail, Attorney Freedman was waiting for me. He just shook his head and said, "You know, Jerry, I could have beaten the armed robbery charge because even though your car was identified, the police still never had any solid evidence on you, since you were wearing a mask, and the attendant couldn't make a positive I.D. But, the one thing I can't justify to a jury is why you were almost three hundred miles away from the Kirksville Jail when you were supposed to be locked up inside that same jail!"

A day or so later, after Freeman had talked it over with the prosecutors, he told me the best he could do was get me five years for everything: armed robbery, escape, and car theft. So I ended up copping a plea, getting a five-year sentence for all that. Since that crime took place in Missouri, I had to pull two years at Jefferson City, the Missouri State Prison, and another two at Menard for violating my parole. I was released from Menard on May 6, 1960, a day I'll never forget as long as I live. I've never been back to prison since.

\*\*\*

Sometime in the late fifties, Mom and her mother, my grandma Mary Maher, pooled their money, moved to St. Louis, and purchased an old, run-down apartment house where they rented out rooms. With all the pressure from Dad leaving, the younger kids having been taken away from her and Jimmy, John and I constantly getting into trouble with the law and doing time, Mom's cross proved too heavy for her to bear. She started drinking again, heavier than ever. She died in 1961, at age 52, from cirrhosis of the liver.

As I mentioned earlier, over the years, there have been several writers who have gone out of their way to portray my family as pure trash. Granted, we were a dysfunctional bunch and scattered to the four winds, but my dad always worked – a darn good mechanic – and my mom also worked until she got so sick with the cirrhosis that she couldn't. In truth, my mom and her whole, pure Irish side of the family, were workaholics. As a matter of fact, even before she and Dad divorced, Mom served as the main breadwinner for our family. I have always been taught that 'trash' refers to people who refuse to work. If that is the case, my family doesn't qualify. Dirt poor, yes, but trash, no.

# CHAPTER TWO

# THE BLOODIEST 47 ACRES IN AMERICA

I suppose I need to back up a few steps to talk about my two years at the Missouri State Penitentiary, also known as "Jeff City," "the bloodiest 47 acres west of the Mississippi," and "the bloodiest 47 acres in America." It was extremely violent during my two years there. The things I had to do to survive had a hell of an impact on my life.

Jeff City had acquired the reputation of being the bloodiest 47 acres in America because of the hundreds of stabbings that had taken place there in the early sixties. In fact, it was so bad that the warden during that time resigned and eventually committed suicide. Also, a major riot had erupted there in the early fifties, not long before I arrived in 1956. Some of the prisoners who had participated were still talking about it when I got there, and they told me what happened.

As does any jail or prison, Jeff City had its convicts who had flipped and turned informant – rats, as the prison population referred to them. When it comes to the status and hierarchy of the penitentiary population, prisoners consider informants the very lowest order. Even compared to mass murderers, rapists and child molesters, informants are the most hated, and therefore the most endangered. If word got out that a prisoner was an informant, he was in constant danger of being murdered. As a rule, the prison officials would move the informant from the main population to Death Row, where security was extra tight, making it virtually impossible to harm them.

I can't remember how, exactly, but at some point, several prisoners at Jeff City managed to overpower the guards and force their way onto Death Row where they yanked all of the informants from their cells and cut out their tongues. This isn't bullshit; this is fact. The incident was written about and documented. From there, the convicts went absolutely crazy, instigating riots that lasted for several days, killing a large number of guards and prisoners in the process. The prison almost burned to the ground! I remember one guy telling me that it was like "taking a bloodbath" because there was so much blood everywhere that you couldn't help but get it all over you. Finally, the prison authorities called in the Missouri Highway Patrol, who helped the guards to bring the riot under control.

Years later, in his book about the King assassination, *The Making of an Assassin*, author George McMillan – I  called him Georgie Pie – said he had talked to a prisoner who had been my brother Jimmy's cellmate at Jeff City. Georgie Pie said the convict/informant had told him that Jimmy, indeed, was a racist. When Jimmy heard about McMillan quoting the informant by name, he laughed. Jimmy rebutted the informant's claim about racism by pointing out that he never had been a cellmate with that particular prisoner. It was well known that the informant had been locked up on Death Row all the time.

During those years, several well-known people did time at Jeff City. World heavyweight boxing champion Sonny Liston was one of them. I can't remember exactly what Liston did to get sentenced to Jeff City (he and I were there at different times), but I do remember an incident in St. Louis involving Liston. Back in those days, the fifties, in St. Louis, practically all of the cops were white. Most of them were crooked as hell! If you think the cops are bad now, they got away with anything and everything back then. If they pulled over a car, the cops would just drag the driver – black or white – out of his car, beat the shit out of him, take his money, and leave him lying there.

Other than my brother Jimmy, probably the best-known person who did time at Jeff City was Charles Arthur Floyd, also known as "Pretty Boy" Floyd, but he was killed before I even was born. However, I met this old-timer at Jeff City, pulling life for murder, who told me that Pretty Boy, after he was released from Jeff City, had worked with the John Dillinger Gang that also included Baby Face Nelson.

\*\*\*

Even though I had been a rough and tumble man prior to arriving at Jeff City, it was the kind of place where I immediately had to up my game as soon as I got there. I was about five-eight and weighed only about 140 pounds. Even though I wasn't all that big, I was fairly quick and packed a pretty good punch for my size. The main thing in my favor, however, was that I didn't back down easily. Uncle Earl had taught me that if anybody ever messed with me for no good reason, to make sure that I evened the score as fast as possible. Uncle Earl always said, "The longer you wait, the worse it gets." I'm not necessarily attempting to glorify Uncle Earl's advice; I'm simply saying I heeded his advice back in those days.

While I was at Jeff City from 1956 to 1958, there were several gangs – black and white – who pretty much ran things inside the prison. However, blacks were segregated from whites to keep down racial conflicts. The main thing all the gangs were interested in was dope – mostly speed and heroin – and also cigarettes, girlie magazines and commissary booklets. Those commodities created the money flow, and whoever controlled the money flow ruled the roost. Once a gang gained control of the money flow, they would bribe the guards who, in return, would cover for that gang so it could remain in control.

However, regardless of how much money a gang had on the books, each prisoner was allowed to spend only fifteen dollars a month. To keep convicts from carrying and exchanging hard cash – guaranteed to lead to serious problems – the prison administration issued commissary coupon books worth fifteen dollars to each prisoner each month. These $15 commissary coupon books allowed them to purchase soda, snacks – stuff like that. Possessing a commissary booklet was therefore practically the same as possessing cash. [Currently, postage stamps serve as currency to inmates, each stamp worth thirty cents.]

When I first got to Jeff City, the worst gang on the inside was a gang run by the Menard Brothers. (And, yes, their last name is spelled the same way as Menard Prison in Illinois, but as far as I know, it's just a coincidence.) The Menard Brothers were two white guys who had this all-white gang of about ten to twelve members, although they changed from time to time. Both Menards were mean as rattlesnakes – kill you over nothing. When we would be out on the yard, the Menard Brothers and their gang packed shanks – prison slang for homemade knives. As they walked around the yard, they held other convicts down and robbed them of anything of any value.

One day, I was standing on one side of the yard with Butch, a guy about my age whom I'd befriended, and we noticed a commotion on the other side of the yard. A big crowd had gathered and everybody was screaming and hollering at the top of their lungs. Suddenly, everything grew quiet, the crowd dispersed, and there was this white convict lying on the ground bleeding badly from a chest wound. Next thing, we heard the bullhorn. The guards rushed onto the yard, herded us inside, and we had a lockdown. Even though there was an investigation, no one would say anything, of course. The truth of the matter is that neither Butch nor I had seen anything because we had been on the other side of the prison yard when the shanking happened. However, word on the yard was that the Menard Brothers had taken down that prisoner because he had stood up against them when they had attempted to steal his belongings. The prisoner that the Menards shanked must have survived because I never heard anything about him dying.

It's important to understand, though, that regardless of the official prison rules set forth by the administration, the only ones that actually count on the inside are those created and set forth by the convicts. One of those rules is that sooner or later you will have to join one of the gangs on the inside. The gangs don't like a prisoner going solo because it demonstrates too much independence, which takes away from total dependence on one of the gangs for survival.

When I arrived at Jeff City, I went to work at the shoe shop, hung out on the yard with Butch, and attempted to mind my business – and only my business. The Menard Gang eventually approached Butch and me about joining. We told them we weren't interested. That didn't sit too well with the Menard Gang because to refuse their offer was to disrespect them. The only way they could get back that respect and maintain control was to catch us out on the yard and take us down in front of the entire population.

I hung with Butch for several reasons. Not only was he smart, cool-headed under pressure and minded his own business, but he was tough as nails. At about five-seven and 190 pounds, he was built like a brick outhouse and was as quick as a cat. I'd heard that Butch was a good fighter, and I was soon to find out just how good he was. Also, he had nerves of steel. Word was out that the Menard Gang was planning to catch Butch and me out on the yard and take us down in front of the prison population because we had refused their offer to join their gang. We decided that we were going to take a stand against the Menard Gang, even if it meant going to an early grave. And, I must admit to you, I was scared to death – all 140 pounds of me!

Butch's job at Jeff City was working in the department that made license plates. In dealing with the Menard Gang, I knew I'd need some sort of advantage, so I had Butch make me a shank out of the metal used to make the license plates. Sneaking a shank past the guards who watched over the license plates crew wasn't easy because the prisoners who made the plates were searched every day when they got off work. Nevertheless, coolheaded Butch managed to do so. I kept the shank – about five inches of handle and five inches of blade – hidden inside my cell for a few days.

The day of our showdown with the Menard Gang was a cold winter day. When it came time to go out on the yard, I put on my prison winter coat, taped the shank's handle, gripped it with my right hand, placed my hands inside my coat pockets and walked out onto the yard. Compared to a normal day out on the yard, where it's usually loud with prisoners talking, trading, working out, playing some kind of ball, or whatever, that particular morning was especially quiet. That's the way it always was when there was going to be a take down on the yard because the convicts were more interested in seeing bloodshed than participating in more productive and less violent activities. It's the prison mindset.

Butch was already out on the yard, smoking a cigarette. The Menard gang was about fifty feet away from Butch. As I walked over to him, I could hear the whispers, and I could practically feel all those intense eyes burning a hole in my back. In our assessment of the Menard Gang, though, Butch and I had noted that the two Menard Brothers who did all the talking and handed out almost all of the beatings for the gang, had one area of vulnerability: they enjoyed hearing their own voices. Before dishing out any physical punishment, each had to give a long-winded speech about how superior he was and how inferior the victim was. The night before, Butch and I had decided that as soon as the shit started going down, Butch would beat one Menard Brother with his fists, and I would shank the other one.

Sure enough, within minutes, the Menard Gang started strolling toward us. As they approached, I saw one Menard whispering to the other. The three Menard brothers came up to us really close and formed a tight circle around us. The rest of the prisoners formed a circle around the Menard Gang, in layers, just like in one of those old westerns where the pioneers pulled their wagons into a circle to defend themselves against an Indian attack.

Just like it had been when the prisoner had been shanked a few weeks before, there was a reason for that: If the guards happened to get wind that something was going down and rushed the yard to stop whatever was going down, they had several circles – layers – of people to go through before making it to the culprits. That way the culprits would have sufficient time to discontinue their crime before being identified because they would be warned by the commotion of the guards struggling to make their way through the circles of convicts.

No one but Butch and I knew that I was packing a shank. However, it was common knowledge to the collective prison population that the Menards always packed shanks. The Menards acted as though they, and only they, had the right to do so.

I must admit that my knees were trembling, and even Butch, tough as he was, also was scared. The oldest and biggest of the Menard brothers said, "What's it gonna be with you two, in or out?" Before his question had time to soak in, all of a sudden, Butch hit the younger Menard brother in the mouth – pop! He went to the ground – out cold. I just stood there, in shock. I think the other Menard brother, the one who'd asked if we were in or out, was also in a state of shock because he, his brother and their gang were not used to anyone taking a stand. Butch had caught them off guard. It wasn't more than a couple of seconds, though, before the other Menard brother made a move towards me. It was now or never, so I came out with the shank. I kind of hugged him, stabbing him in the stomach with it as hard as I could, and started pulling up. (Another prisoner, who watched the whole ordeal, later told me that it sounded like someone ripping open a 100-pound burlap bag of corn) He let out a loud Uhhhh!, froze in place, and his eyeballs looked as though they were going to pop out of his head. I pulled out the shank, and, in all honesty, just stood there for a second watching him bleed. I heard somebody holler, "Stick him again!" I reared back with the shank and took aim, more out of fright than anything else.

Suddenly, the bullhorn sounded, and someone hollered, "Guards!" Butch quickly grabbed the shank from me. Several other prisoners gathered closer around us, while Butch passed the shank to one of them, who passed it to another, and so on down the line, from prisoner to prisoner. That was so the guards couldn't confiscate the assault weapon. Of course, the guards asked everybody what had happened, who had done what to whom, but, naturally, no one had heard or seen anything. Luckily, I didn't have enough blood on me to get the guards' attention. Actually, there was a light snow that day, and since I was wearing a dark colored winter jacket, what little blood I did have on me just sort of blended in with the moisture created by the snowfall. For the record, Menard wasn't killed.

Quite honestly, the guards didn't press too hard about who had assaulted the Menards because the guards themselves were glad to see the brothers get their asses kicked, as big a pain in the ass as they were. For several months, both Butch and I slept with one eye open because we knew there would be a payback. However, after that day, many of the prisoners rallied around Butch and me because they too were tired of taking shit from the Menards. In spite of how fierce the fight had been, we all survived the incident.

From that day forward, the Menards didn't bother us, and we didn't bother them. Plus, the Menards didn't bother anyone who hung with Butch and me. It wasn't as though we had a gang of our own, but we had established ourselves, and we now had respect out on the prison yard. The numbers were on our side and the tide was flowing in our favor. That day on the yard with the Menards was a turning point in my life – both good and bad. The incident gave me a sense of self-confidence, but over the following years, that fearlessness could have killed me.

\*\*\*

By this time, Jimmy had already gone to prison three times: in California, 1949 to 1950, for breaking into that business office; Pontiac Prison, 1952 to 1954, for robbing a Chicago cab driver; and Leavenworth Federal Prison, 1955 to 1958, for his involvement with Walter Rife in that money order scam. However, sometime in the fall of 1959, during my incarceration at Menard Prison, I found out that Jimmy and another ex-con, James Owens, had been arrested for robbing a Kroger's Store in St. Louis. Jimmy received a 20-year sentence for robbing that store. He was processed into Jeff City sometime during March 1960, just before I was released from Menard on May 6, 1960.

As noted earlier, I didn't see much of my family from 1950 through 1967 because I was locked up most of that period. I saw even less of Jimmy from 1950 until 1967 because one or both of us were usually on the inside during that entire time frame. However, Jimmy did visit me once while I was at Menard between 1958 and 1960. It happened that Jimmy was free and on the outside for a good portion of that particular period, while both John and me were locked up inside Menard.

Most of what I know about Jimmy's time spent inside Jeff City – from early 1960 through spring 1967 – came to me from a man named J.J. Maloney, whom I spoke with on more than one occasion during that period.

When Jimmy arrived at Jeff City towards the beginning of 1960 for robbing the Kroger's Store in St. Louis, J.J. Maloney was already serving time at Jeff City. Maloney was only nineteen years old at the time and he was serving four life sentences for armed robbery and murder. Even though Maloney was from St. Louis, and Jimmy had spent a considerable amount of time in the St. Louis area, they weren't personally acquainted with each other prior to being incarcerated together at Jeff City. However, as Maloney told me, he and Jimmy did know some of the same people from the St. Louis area.

Some writers have attempted to make Jimmy out a racist, hard drinker, drug user and sexual deviate. In his book *Killing the Dream*, Gerald Posner alleges that Jimmy was guilty of all of the above, saying that Jimmy not only used and sold amphetamines – speed – but made a lot of money from such trafficking. Posner claims that Jimmy sent those illicit earning to John and me, and that we stashed away that money for him.

Well, Maloney told me that during the time frame he was incarcerated at Jeff City – which overlapped with the entire time Jimmy was there – Maloney and Jimmy were around each other quite a bit, even though they didn't talk to each other all that much. They had both – separately – attempted to escape from Jeff City, and because of these attempts, they would be relocated to a more secure area of the prison and that is where they got acquainted. If my recollection serves me well from my time at Jeff City, those who attempted an escape were housed in E-Hall.

Maloney later told me that while he was doing time inside Jeff City, he (Maloney) used and trafficked amphetamines – and heavily! He said he knew everyone who used and sold amphetamines, and that never at any time did he see my brother purchase, use, or sell amphetamines. [According to my older brother, John, Jeff City now gives tours in which they include the fact that James Earl Ray was a prisoner there, and also the fact that he never did use or sell drugs in prison.]

While on the inside, most prisoners – those with any ambition that is – have a small business going on, something on the side, to pick up some extra money. Maloney revealed to me that, for a while, Jimmy ran a magazine stand, renting out magazines like True Detective and Argosy to the prisoners. Magazines like that were popular at that time. Maloney made a special point to tell me that Jimmy didn't carry 'girlie' magazines on his stand because carrying such magazines – although they were by far the most popular – required that you do business with a bad element. This was sure to land you in hot water. Maloney told me that Jimmy had said to him one day on the yard: "You can't fuck with a bunch of sex freaks and hope for anything good."

In addition to Posner's false claims about Jimmy, another writer created false stories about Jimmy, too. Writer George

McMillan – in his book *The Making of an Assassin* – attempted to portray Jimmy as the worst kind of racist. McMillan's claims became the basis for a feature story about Jimmy in the January 26, 1976 issue of *Time* magazine. The article, "The King Assassination Revisited," drew heavily from the following material in McMillan's book:

> In 1963 and 1964, Martin Luther King was on TV almost every day talking defiantly about how black people were going to get their rights, insisting they would accept with nonviolence all the terrible violence that white people were inflicting on them until the day of victory arrived, until they did overcome. Ray watched it all avidly on the cellblock TV at Jeff City. He reacted as if King's remarks were directed at him personally. He boiled when King came on the tube; he began to call him Martin "Lucifer" King and Martin Luther "Coon." It got so that the very sight of King would galvanize Ray. "Somebody's gotta get him," Ray would say, his face drawn with tension, his fists clenched. "Somebody's gotta get him."[1]

However, J.J. Maloney – who was, after all, at Jeff City during this same period – told me that George McMillan was guilty of a serious blunder when he made these statements and levied these allegations. Maloney said that there were no cellblock televisions in Jeff City the whole period James Earl Ray was an inmate there, from early 1960 through spring 1967. It wasn't until late 1970 that cellblock televisions were allowed at Jeff City. Prison officials can corroborate this. Therefore, the so-called "evidence" that Jimmy was a racist proved completely false. McMillan had no basis for his statements at all.

Also, as Maloney described to me, there had been serious repercussions from the allegations by writers such as McMillan about Jimmy's alleged drug use and alleged drug sales while inside Jeff City. As I mentioned, some writers stated that Jimmy

---

1     George McMillan, *The Making on an Assassin: The Life of James Earl Ray* (Boston: Little, Brown and Company, 1976); J.J. Maloney, "James Earl Ray," Crime Magazine, an Encyclopedia of Crime.
http://www.crimemagazine.com/Assassinations/james.htm (accessed 9 February 2009).

had not only made profits from trafficking amphetamines while inside Jeff City, but also that Jimmy had somehow allegedly managed to get those proceeds from the alleged drug trafficking to us, his family. Furthermore, that we had allegedly stashed it away for him. Finally, those same government writers alleged that Jimmy, once he escaped from Jeff City, had used those proceeds to finance his travels, and to stalk and kill King.

These allegations caused tremendous turbulence amongst Missouri's high-ranking politicians and those in charge of the Missouri Prison System. They certainly didn't want to go down in history as having allegedly allowed James Earl Ray to profit from dealing drugs inside Jeff City and to have used those profits toward stalking and killing Martin Luther King, not only a strong voice for the plight of the black people, but arguably the most influential civil rights leader ever.

Things heated up so much for the state of Missouri that Reverend Emanuel Cleaver, who then served as the executive director of the Kansas City Chapter of the Southern Christian Leadership Conference, requested that Missouri Governor Christopher Boyd open an investigation into these allegations. This would have been in the mid-1970s.

George M. Camp, head of the Missouri prison system, became involved and Camp, indeed, conducted his own inquiry. After talking with author George McMillan, Camp got back to Cleaver with the following response:

> My findings are that there is nothing whatsoever to substantiate any conclusion that James Earl Ray either financed his escape or activities after his escape through any means while he was an inmate at the Missouri State Penitentiary. During the six years that James Earl Ray was an inmate at the Missouri State Penitentiary, he kept primarily to himself and, other than for the fact that he attempted to escape on more than one occasion, he had only one conduct violation during that entire time and that was the possession of three packages of cigarettes, a ball point pen and one pound of coffee … In addition, you might be interested to know that

prior to the Governor's receiving your mailgram, I personally discussed the allegations and the conclusions in the
Time magazine article with the author himself, Mr. George
McMillan. In the course of our conversation, I pressed him
for details regarding drug sales or any other illegal activities
in which staff and/or inmates might have been involved. He
[McMillan] was unable to give me any specifics but just responded that it was common knowledge.[2]

I mentioned this merely to yet again illustrate how the prosecutors, government and their writers had tried – and still are
trying – and at any length, regardless of facts pointing to the
contrary, to portray my brother Jimmy as a drug dealer and
a racist who murdered Martin Luther King because of some
racial hatred towards him.

J.J. Maloney also told me that during the nearly seven years
that he was around Jimmy at Jeff City, he never witnessed Jimmy conduct himself in any way that would have indicated he
was a racist of any kind.

Before moving on, I want to explain why I would use J.J.
Maloney, an ex-convict who did prison time for armed robbery and murder, as a source of credible information. Here's
the answer:

While in prison for thirteen years at Jeff City, Maloney not
only overcame his drug habits, but he educated himself and
developed a strong command of the King's English. Even while
doing time at Jeff City, Maloney became a book reviewer for
the *Kansas City Star* newspaper. Maloney was paroled in 1972
and immediately went to work as a reporter for the *Kansas
City Star*. By 1973, Maloney was working as a full-time reporter for that newspaper.

Between his release from Jeff City in 1972, and his death in
1999, reformed convict/journalist J.J. Maloney received far too
many literary awards to list here. However, to give you an idea
of his greatness, I will list a few examples. During his career,
J.J. Maloney was:

2          J.J. Maloney, "James Earl Ray," Crime Magazine, an Encyclopedia of Crime,
http://www.crimemagazine.com/Assassinations/james.htm (accessed 9 February 2009).

- nominated for the Pulitzer Prize five times;
- awarded the American Bar Association's highest award, The Silver Gavel;
- awarded the American Society of Newspaper Publishers' prize for the Best Investigative Story;
- author of five published books – fiction, non-fiction and poetry.

No doubt, there will be some who will attempt to discredit me for utilizing J.J. Maloney as a source of information, but if it is true that anyone is capable of being rehabilitated after a life of crime, it is obviously the case concerning the late J.J. Maloney.

# CHAPTER THREE

# BIGGER STAKES

When I was released from Menard on May 6, 1960, I caught the bus to St. Louis because by then, my whole family had moved there. When I arrived at the St. Louis Bus Station, Catman Gawron was waiting for me. I'd been locked up for four years, so he bought me a lot of beer and I got drunk as hell – had a splitting headache the next morning.

As noted earlier, Catman and Mom were in a relationship at that time. Meanwhile, Mom and Grandma Maher had purchased the old rental house on Hickory Street in St. Louis, although Mom had sold out her part to Grandma and had moved to a house on Mississippi Street. Never one to turn her back on her kids, Mom let me move in with her for a while. My brother John was staying with Mom too. He'd been released from Menard in February 1960, a couple months before I was released on May 6, 1960.

Soon after I arrived in St. Louis, John and I got a job picking strawberries in Kentucky, so we went down there for a couple weeks and when the strawberry job was over in Kentucky, John went to Michigan to pick strawberries. Having had my fill of strawberries, literally and figuratively, I returned to St. Louis. For quite a while, I didn't do much of anything.

After John finished picking strawberries, he went to Arlington Heights, Illinois, a suburb of Chicago, where he got a job as a bartender at the Rolling Green Country Club. He kept calling and telling me that if I could just make it to Arlington Heights, he could get me a job at Rolling Green. I was flat broke and I wasn't about to let a small problem like that stop me from landing a good job.

I had been casing out this drugstore in St. Louis for a couple weeks, but decided I needed some help. I contacted a friend named Smitty who had done time with me at Jeff City. I knew he was reliable and would keep his mouth shut. In August 1960, Smitty and I – using the standard M.O. of mask over head and revolver in hand – robbed the drug store and made off with about $400.00. I took my share and caught a train from St. Louis to Arlington Heights, Illinois. Sure enough, just as he'd promised, John got me a job at the Rolling Green Country Club – a high-end club. That's where I initiated my career as a country club attendant, a line of work I would continue, off and on, for the remainder of my working years.

My job at Rolling Green was that of "houseman," just a glorified term for 'gofer' and janitor. As houseman, my job was to sweep, vacuum, take out the garbage, and do general cleaning. I remained at Rolling Green Country Club until the first part of 1962. At that point, the manager at Rolling Green landed a better job at North Shore Country Club in Glenview, Illinois and because I had done a good job for him at Rolling Green, he took me with him to North Shore. My job title at North Shore Country Club was "locker-room attendant." Best damn legal money I ever made in my life! Working country clubs in the sixties, you generally received a salary along with room and board. This was the case at North Shore. In addition, during the summertime the golf courses were full almost everyday and I averaged about $300 a week in tips. My salary was $380.00 per month, or $95.00 per week. But, during the summer months at North Shore, I was making approximately $395.00 per week. In 1962, $395.00 per week was more money than most doctors and lawyers made.

During my time at Rolling Green Country Club, I had been romantically involved with a girl named Carol Sartin. She had become pregnant by me – a real no-no back in those days.

Dressed in her maternity clothes, minus a wedding band, Carol moved back to her hometown near Knoxville, Tennessee to have our child, a boy, in May of 1962. She named him Michael Ray even though Carol and I never married. After Michael was born, sometime in 1962, I gave up my job at North Shore Country Club and traveled to Morristown, Tennessee, to visit my son for a few days.

I returned to Chicago and the employment agency sent me to the Olympia Fields Country Club in another suburb of Chicago. I was hired as a "cook's helper." The U.S. Open Golf Tournament was sometimes held at Olympia Fields, a very high level country club. It was August 1963, and I had been at Olympia Fields for about three weeks when I received a sad call from John. Our younger brother Frank had been killed in a car wreck. I quit Olympia Fields Country Club and made my way to Quincy, Illinois to attend Frank's funeral ... one of the saddest days in my life. Also, Frank's funeral was the last time I ever saw my sister Susan. After Frank's funeral, we just lost touch. She got married and moved to Chicago somewhere. As a matter of fact, my brother John and I just found out that Susan died in 1994, in Houston Texas. She was only 47 years old. When she was young, she could have been a model. Maybe, one day, I will get to see Susan again.

*\*\**

Sometime in 1963, on one of my trips to St. Louis to visit John, I ran into Butch, the tough guy I had served time with at Jeff City, and a buddy of his, a big, tall, Native American guy. Since you couldn't legally buy liquor in St. Louis, Missouri on a Sunday, all four of us hopped into the car and drove across the bridge into East St. Louis, Illinois, where you could. We went inside a tavern and proceeded to knock back several drinks.

My brother John was pretty cocky when he got a few in him, and he walked up to this pretty young girl, put his arm around her, and flirted with her. Little did John know, she had a jealous boyfriend watching the whole time. The boyfriend confronted John and a fight broke out. Three or four men jumped on John, and I jumped in to help my brother. About that time, somebody busted a beer bottle over my head and good old Butch came in hard and fast – pop! pop! – and nailed a couple of the guys we were fighting with, ending the fight. I was bleeding like a stuck hog because they split my head wide open, and John's eye was nearly swollen shut. Butch's girlfriend was a nurse or in nursing school and she patched me up as best she could. I have never seen Butch again since that day.

After we buried Frank, I went back to the employment agency in Chicago. I got a job at the Medinah Country Club in Medinah, Illinois, another place where the U.S. Open had been held. My job title at Medinah was "gate keeper." I checked the members in and out at the gate entrance to the club. While employed at Medinah, I walked everywhere I went. Usually, when I would get off work, I would walk to a store up the street, buy a newspaper and a couple of beers, then walk back to my living quarters at the Medinah Country Club. One night in January of 1964, while walking back to my quarters after getting my beer and newspaper, I was struck by a car and nearly killed. I broke my pelvic bone and received a serious concussion, remaining unconscious for about three days. The doctor told me that if I hadn't been young and healthy, I surely would have died.

John drove from St. Louis to Medinah to get me and take me back to St. Louis with him. I stayed with John until I healed and then I went back again to the employment agency in Chicago – old faithful. I landed a job as "grounds keeper" at the Sportsman's Country Club in Northbrook, near Chicago, and worked there until late 1965 and after a while became "grounds keeper/custodian." I got paid extra for performing the custodial duties.

During my years working country clubs around Illinois, from approximately 1960 to 1992, I never was late and didn't even miss a single day of work, except one day in 1988 when

I was working at the Onwentsia Country Club in Lake Forest, Illinois, and my boss made me go home because I had the flu. That was the only day I missed work during all those years. So much for me being lazy and shiftless.

During the early to mid sixties, while Jimmy was doing time at Jeff City for the Kroger's robbery, I had come to believe that he would never make it out of there. First off, Jeff City was so violent that a convict's life could be decided on nothing more a shift in the wind, the wrong look or a depressing letter from home. Secondly, since Jimmy was in his late thirties and pushing forty, and doing twenty years, I felt that time, if nothing else, would claim him. However, I also knew that Jimmy had no intention of spending his remaining years locked up inside Jeff City. An escape always loomed as a possibility.

From 1966 to 1967, John was able to visit Jimmy at Jeff City more than I was because he lived and worked much closer to Jefferson City than I did. On April 24, 1967, I got a call from John and Jimmy together, reporting that Jimmy had busted out of Jeff City! Jimmy had attempted to escape Jeff City a couple of other times but had been unsuccessful. John had Jimmy with him. They wanted me to catch a train into Chicago and meet them at the Fairview Hotel on South Michigan Avenue downtown.

Jimmy recounts in his book that after he escaped from Jeff City on April 23, he hid for several days, then jumped a freight train into St. Louis, and attempted to locate Catman Gawron. After failing to locate Catman, he went to Chicago and in May, he landed a job as a dishwasher at the Indian Trails Restaurant in the suburb of Winnetka.[1] The reason Jimmy told the story with so much detail was that he didn't want to implicate John and me.

However, the truth is that I did catch a train from Northbrook to Chicago on April 24, 1967 and I did spend time together with Jimmy and John at the Fairview Hotel in Chicago. Since Jimmy and John were already waiting in the room, I just went straight up to it. Jimmy looked pretty rough, limping around and several

1      James Earl Ray, *Tennessee Waltz: The Making of a Political Prisoner* (Saint Andrews, Tennessee: Saint Andrew's Press, 1987), 42-43.

pounds thinner than when I'd last seen him. Immediately, my two brothers told me what had happened.

Prior to his escape, Jimmy had a job inside Jeff City working in the prison bakery that supplied fresh bread for the entire prison population serving at Jeff City. Two satellite farms, called 'honor farms' because the less dangerous prisoners worked there, provided fresh vegetables to that prison population. Every day, the trucks from the satellite farms transported fresh produce inside Jeff City, and every day, several trucks transported freshly baked bread from Jeff City to the satellite farms on the outside.

On the morning of April 23, 1967, Jimmy, carrying a pair of black civilian pants, hid in the false bottom of a large breadbox, and some fellow convicts covered him with loaves of bread. The guards unknowingly loaded the breadbox containing my brother onto the truck. En route to the satellite farms, Jimmy quietly made his way out of the breadbox to the back door and jumped off the truck onto the ground – his first taste of freedom in seven years.

John had visited Jimmy on the day before he escaped, and they had a designated spot where John was suppose to pick Jimmy up. However, for whatever reason, they ended up getting their wires crossed. John was not at the designated place when Jimmy arrived. Since he figured the prison authorities would be hunting him, Jimmy walked a long way down the railroad tracks, hoping no one would see him, until he finally found a telephone. He got hold of John and John went back and picked up Jimmy. That's why Jimmy's feet were so sore: He'd walked down the railroad tracks in those thin prison shoes. John and Jimmy didn't reach Chicago until the following day, April 24, 1967.

The three of us went out and brought some food, beer and whiskey, and brought it all back to the room at the Fairview Hotel where we spent the day. That night, after John and I gave Jimmy about a hundred dollars each, I caught a train back to Northbrook, so I could report for work at 11 p.m. that night and

John drove back to St. Louis. Jimmy rented a cheap room somewhere just outside Chicago, so he could let his feet heal.

That day at the Fairview Hotel, April 24, 1967, was the first time in almost twenty years that Jimmy, John and I had been in the same room together. Sadly enough, it would be the last time, we three brothers would ever be together in a free setting.

A week or so later, Jimmy called me at the Sportsman's Country Club and told me he had gotten a job as dishwasher at the Indian Trails Restaurant in Winnetka. It was not far from Northbrook, so about once a week, Jimmy and I would get together and shoot some pool, throw a couple of cold ones down the hatch and keep each other posted on what was going on.

During that time, Jimmy told me something that has never been revealed before. He wanted to make his way into Canada. He told me that he was going to attempt to acquire a false identification, hook up with the Merchant Marines, and possibly make his way out of America, into one of those countries in Africa like the Belgian Congo, and hire on as a mercenary. He said, "Brother, I'm thirty-nine years old, and not only do I have thirteen years of a twenty-year sentence remaining to be served at Jeff City, I also have an additional five for the prison escape. Hell, if I'm ever caught and have to go back and do that much time, I'll be almost sixty years old before I'm out. I believe I'll take my chances in another country."

However, Jimmy needed not just a ride, but money with which to make his way into Canada. I was making fairly good money at the Sportsman's Country Club and Jimmy had saved a few dollars working at the Indian Trails Restaurant, but even combining the two, it wasn't enough money for what he had in mind. I told Jimmy I had an idea.

There was a poker game in downtown Chicago almost every night, not too far off South Michigan Avenue, in an old abandoned bar. The game was hosted and run by a local tough guy named Jess – big guy. I had attended and played the game a couple times. Usually there were anywhere from eight to twelve players. It had been about two months, though, since

I'd been there. This wasn't a high stakes game, but it wasn't a chump-change game either. Sometimes the pots reached a few thousand dollars.

One evening early in July 1967, around 11:00 p.m. on a Thursday – my only night off from work – Jimmy and I took a train to Chicago. I carried an overnight bag with me. Inside the bag were a .38 Special, a sawed-off baseball bat and two ski masks. Back in those days, a .38 Special was about the easiest handgun to come by on the street.

During the short train ride to Chicago, I told Jimmy how the deal would go down. I knew that Jess, the guy who ran the game, always had a .45 automatic stuck down inside his belt. And, it made common sense that some of the other players would be packing, too. Jess always manned the door and monitored who was allowed in and who was turned away. You had to drop a familiar name to get Jess to open the door. When I had attended the game the first time, I had gone with a friend named Stoney, but he was doing time. However, I had noticed that there was a man named Luke who was obviously a regular player there.

Jimmy and I disembarked in Chicago, made our way to the gambling den, and put on our ski masks. Jimmy carried the .38 Special and I had a sawed-off baseball bat. We knocked on the door and, sure enough, Jess asked, "Who is it?" I can't remember what name I gave Jess, but I do remember that I told him I was a friend of Luke's. I could hear mumbling on the other side, so I figured Jess was asking Luke if he was familiar with the name I had given. However, Jess made a fatal mistake … he cracked open the door. I looked at Jimmy and nodded. We rushed the door, knocking Jess to the floor. Jess was already reaching for his .45, but before he could get it from his waistband, I swatted him in the arm with the baseball bat. Jimmy already had the .38 pointed at the other players – about seven of them, as I remember – and told them not to move or he'd shoot the first one who did. I grabbed the .45 from Jess, backhanded him in the nose with it, and then aimed it at the players sitting at the card table. We ordered all of them to put their hands in the air so we could see them. They complied without hesitation. Sure enough, Luke was among the players.

While Jimmy kept the .38 trained on the table, I scooped all the loose cash already on the table into the overnight bag. I then ordered all of them to lay their wallets and jewelry on the table. As they did so, I raked all of that into the overnight bag. I told everyone to stand up so I could frisk them. It was a good thing I patted them down because I took a .25 automatic off one guy and a .32 revolver off another. We made them get down on their stomachs, and then we rushed out of there.

Jimmy and I caught the train back to Northbrook where we split our takings – a little over $1,800.00 in cash and a few pieces of fairly nice jewelry, rings, watches, plus some extra handguns – a .45, a .32 and a .25. Jimmy took his cut – a little over $900.00, and bought a used 1962 Plymouth.

There's something I need to mention here.

When the House Select Committee on Assassinations (HSCA) met in the mid-late seventies to review the Martin Luther King and John Fitzgerald Kennedy assassinations, they tried their best to connect the Ray brothers – Jimmy, John and me – to the Alton, Illinois bank robbery of July 1967. That bank robbery reportedly netted around $27,000.00. The HSCA's primary objective was to connect James Earl Ray to the Alton Bank robbery, convince the public that his cut was around $9,000.00, and then convince the public that James Earl Ray used the $9,000.00 to finance stalking and killing King. For the record, we did not rob the Alton Bank! I even took a lie detector test for F. Lee Bailey about this – and I passed.

So, Jimmy left for Canada in that used Plymouth in July 1967. (Just think: If Jimmy had participated in the Alton Bank robbery and had received $9,000.00 as his cut, he would have purchased a more dependable car than a used 1962 Plymouth.) In all honesty, I didn't know whether I'd ever see Jimmy again. I figured if he happened to make it to one of those African countries, there was no telling what would become of him. But sometime around late August or early September 1967, I got a call from Jimmy – it was on a Thursday, my day off. He told me to catch a train to Chicago and not to drive because he had returned from Canada and he was going to give me his old Plymouth. After I got off work the next day, I caught a train to Chicago and met Jimmy at some hotel downtown, the name of which I cannot recall. Once we settled down in our hotel room, Jimmy said we were going out on the town, money was no problem, and he was going to pay for everything.

And did we ever go out on the town! We went to some fancy steak house and had a couple of Porter House steaks with all the trimmings. We then hit a couple of clubs and had a few drinks, even though Jimmy rarely drank alcohol. As we were making our way back to the hotel room, Jimmy found us a couple of fine-looking hookers, and we took them back to the hotel room.

The next morning, Jimmy and I checked out of the room, got in his Plymouth, and headed down to the Chicago Train Station. Even though none of us brothers ever had been in the habit of nosing into one another's business, I asked Jimmy, as he was about to board the train, what he was going to be doing from here on out. He told me that while in Canada, he'd met a smuggler named "Raoul," and that he'd be working for Raoul for a while. I didn't ask Jimmy what kind of work he was going to do for Raoul, but I figured it had to be some kind of smuggling, either dope or guns, or both. That was the first time I ever heard the name Raoul – a name that has caused me grief over the years, and continues to cause me grief to this very day.

As Jimmy was boarding the train (for Birmingham, Alabama), he handed me the keys to his Plymouth. He said there were still some of his things inside the Plymouth and in a few days, he wanted me to mail them general delivery to him at the Birmingham Post Office in care of Eric S. Galt. He told me that from then on, he would be going by that alias. Jimmy got on the train, and I got in his car and drove it back to Northbrook. A couple of days later, I mailed Jimmy's things to the Birmingham Post Office in the name of Eric S. Galt. There may still be some postal records that can prove that.

[A lot has been said and written about Jimmy's many aliases. Even as children, we all grew up with a father who changed his last name every time we moved because of his jail time. Jimmy always used names of people he knew or composites of his family names. However, after the King assassination, four of his five aliases were names of Canadian citizens living near Toronto. My brother did not know these men and had never traveled to Toronto. There were three of them that Jimmy used – Paul Bridgeman, Ramon George Sneyd and Eric Starvo Galt. At the HSCA hearings, Chief Council Richard Sprague asked Jimmy, "Now, do you have any idea how you happened to pick that name [Eric Starvo Galt]?"

Jimmy responded, "I could have gotten it out of a phone book, or anything. It's something that I'd remember and it could have been, the names could have been from several different sources. I can't specifically say."

My brother's answers seemed strange. We all thought so. The HSCA concluded that the Toronto aliases were "a matter of primary interest because of the almost unbelievable nature of the coincidences involved." *And* they doubted Jimmy's ability to come up with them. Here are just a few of these strange "coincidences":

- They had similar physical appearances – height, weight, build, etc. Jimmy, Willard and Galt all had facial scars.
- Galt, Sneyd and Bridgeman all lived in Scarborough, a suburb of Toronto, within 1-¾ miles of each other.
- Several months before the assassination, Galt had plastic surgery on the tip of his nose. Four months before the assassination, my brother had the exact same surgery.
- Jimmy styled his hair like these men did, which was not like him.

How did Jimmy find these aliases? I don't see how he could have. But, official investigators never proposed any credible alternative explanation. The HSCA concluded that even though the coincidences were "remarkable" and "almost" unbelievable, they were just that – coincidences.

The odd thing was that both Jimmy and the HSCA denied the most logical possibility – that a person or persons involved in the murder of MLK provided him the aliases. My brother couldn't have found those names. They were provided for him! The man in Toronto named Eric S. Galt worked for Union Carbide of Canada, Ltd. He did highly secret work. He had a high security clearance. This company was 75% American owned. Jimmy had no contact with Union Carbide, never lived or worked in Toronto. I think the use of these names was a way to get Jimmy involved in a conspiracy without him realizing what was going on.]

Between that day at the Chicago train station in late August or early September 1967 – when I first heard about Raoul and Jimmy gave me the keys to his Plymouth – until April 4, 1968, Jimmy called me three times. Each time, I could hear him dropping in the coins into the pay phone, and the calls were fairly short, lasting only about three minutes before the money would run out and "click," that would be it.

***

April 4, 1968 happened to be on a Thursday, always my day off at the Sportsman's Country Club. Since I worked six days per week, I was usually worn out from it and would hang around the club and rest up. That day I was inside my room at the Club watching television when a news bulletin broke in and said that Reverend Dr. Martin Luther King, Jr. had been shot in Memphis, Tennessee. I didn't give it much thought. Even though I wasn't happy about King getting shot, I didn't pay very much attention to the Civil Rights Movement, and didn't have any real interest in it, one way or the other. Later that night the news said that King had died.

There were televisions all over the Sportsman's place, and regardless of what area I was working in, I had constant visual access to the news. Since April 4th, the King assassination had been all-day, every day headline news because rioting had broken out everywhere and authorities were still looking for King's killer. Suddenly, there was a newsflash: it was an update concerning the true identity of the assassin of Reverend Dr. Martin Luther King, Jr. I stopped working and listened. What! ? Surely not....

Jerry Ray in 1966.
Photo courtesy of Jerry Ray.

# CHAPTER FOUR

# WILL THE REAL RAOUL PLEASE STAND UP!

I stopped what I was doing and moved closer to the nearest television set. The news bulletin was saying that authorities were searching for a man named Eric S. Galt – or maybe Eric Starvo Galt, I can't remember exactly which – in connection with the assassination of Reverend Dr. Martin Luther King, Jr. I just sort of froze in place and looked around. They're talking about Jimmy!, I thought to myself. I don't remember the exact day that I heard about Eric S. Galt on the television, just that it was a couple of weeks after the King assassination. Old news clips say that the media first announced on April 17, 1968 that authorities were looking for Galt, so I suppose that's probably the day I heard about it.

\*\*\*

A white (actually a very pale yellow – a color called 'Spring Time Yellow') 1966 Mustang had been found abandoned at the Capitol Homes Housing Project in Atlanta, Georgia, on April 11, 1968. Since a 1966 Mustang had been identified at the scene of the King assassination in Memphis, there was a nationwide alert for that car. The Atlanta Police Department suspected that the Mustang found at Capitol Homes Housing Project was linked to the King assassination and so the FBI was immediately called in.

Don Wilson, a 25 year-old agent with the Atlanta FBI office, was one of two agents who made the initial response. While the senior agent conferred with Atlanta Police, Wilson opened the driver's side door and two pieces of paper fell out. Thinking the papers were insignificant and that possibly he had messed up a crime scene, Wilson stashed the two pieces of paper inside his pocket. It was not until later that Wilson discovered the great significance of the two pieces of paper: they had the name "Raoul" written on them, plus other information. Realizing the racist attitudes of the Atlanta FBI Office, Wilson decided not to turn over the two pieces of paper because he feared they would be discarded, discounted or disposed of altogether.

***

At the Sportsman's, I worked the graveyard shift, 11 p.m. until 7 a.m. As soon as I got off work at 7 a.m. on Thursday after hearing that the law was searching for Eric S. Galt, I jumped in my car and headed for St. Louis. It took me about seven hours from the Club in Northbrook, Illinois to St. Louis was about a seven-hour drive, back in those days, anyway, before all the modern four-lanes they now have.

By this time, April 1968, John had opened a bar called the Grapevine Tavern, a wild place on 1982 Arsenal Street in St. Louis. Since John was a convicted felon, the liquor license was in the name of a family member. When I finally arrived, I pulled John off to the side so we could talk in private, away from the customers. I asked him if he had been following the news about the King assassination. He said that he had because it was constantly on the news. I then asked if he'd heard that the authorities were now looking for Eric S. Galt in connection with King's murder. John nonchalantly said that he'd heard something about somebody named Galt. I stuck my face close to John's face, and, in a low tone, said, "John, Eric S. Galt is our brother, Jimmy." John blurted out, "What the hell are you talking about?!" I said,

"Calm down and listen to me." I then told John about Jimmy giving me his car, and telling me at the Chicago train station that from then on he would be going by the alias Eric. S. Galt. John just shook his head and said, "Holy shit!"

After telling John that Galt was Jimmy, and agreeing to keep it between us, I jumped back in my car and drove back to North-brook so I could report to work at the Sportsman's. Although I barely made it back in time, I went back to work as though nothing had happened. Then, a couple days later while I was watching television as I usually did before my shift at 11 p.m., there was another news flash about the King assassination: after supposedly cross-checking fingerprints taken at the scene of the King assassination against those on file, the FBI had concluded that Eric Starvo Galt was an alias being used by James Earl Ray, an escaped convict from the Missouri State Penitentiary. Now they were searching for James Earl Ray – Jimmy!

I got dressed and waited for them to show up. In less than an hour, there was a knock on my door. I opened the door, and, sure enough, there stood the men in black – the FBI. They said they wanted me to come downtown with them and answer some questions. They took me to their headquarters in downtown Chicago and interrogated me for quite a while, asking me questions about Jimmy that you would expect: When was the last time I'd seen or spoken to him? Did I know anything about the King murder? Did I have anything to do with the King murder? They also asked questions about various members of my family.

There is one thing I told the FBI that night that I would like to clear up – right here and now. Jimmy eventually told them the same story, and both Jimmy and I have been misrepresent-ed concerning it. I told the FBI that both our mom and dad were dead, when, in fact, our dad, George Ray, was still alive and well. He didn't pass away until 1985, at the age of eighty-five. The reason I told the FBI such, and the reason Jimmy told them the same thing, was that our dad was a parole violator, a fugitive from justice, and we didn't want to see him go back to prison, especially at his age.

The FBI finally let me go that day, telling me they were going to monitor me very closely, and I knew they damn well would. Actually, for several weeks straight, the FBI picked me up at work, transported me to headquarters in downtown Chicago, and interrogated me about Jimmy and the King assassination.

After it became public news that the FBI was looking for James Earl Ray in connection with the King assassination, and that I was his brother, the media was intent on talking to me. At that point, however, no one connected to the media knew precisely where I was living or where I was working. Of course, the FBI knew where I was, and it was only a matter of time before they passed on that information to one of their "friendly" reporters, as they referred to them.

There were three main newspapers in Chicago back then, the *Chicago Tribune*, the *Chicago Daily News* and the *Chicago Sun Times*. The *Sun Times* had a well-known crime and mob reporter named Art Petacque. Chicago was a haven for high profile mobsters, maybe more so than any other city in the United States. It had been the headquarters for Al Capone and Bugs Moran. More recently, during the fifties and early sixties, Sam Giancana had been the mob boss of Chicago. I used to read a lot about Giancana – including assertions that he'd had a hand in everything from the St. Valentine's Day Massacre, to fixing the 1960 presidential election so Kennedy could win, to the murder of Marilyn Monroe, to assassination attempts on Fidel Castro. I imagine there is a degree of truth to some of those stories. There even has floated around a story that our dad was involved in the St. Valentine's Day Massacre. Now, that's a bunch of bull!

Nevertheless, Art Petacque was known as the 'main man' when it came to newspaper reporting on high-level crime in the Chicago area. A couple of days after the media revealed that James Earl Ray was wanted in connection with the King assassination, I was in my room at the Sportsman's when there was a knock on my door. I wanted to dodge the media for as long as I could, so I cautiously went to the door and asked who it was. The voice on the other side said he was the deputy sheriff and he needed to talk to me. I unlocked the door and opened it as far as the safety latch would allow. A hand reached through, showing a deputy sheriff's badge. Thinking everyone was legit I went ahead and opened the door. Lo and behold, there stood Art Petacque with a cameraman right behind him. Immediately, a flash blinded me as the photographer snapped a shot of me in my underwear, standing in the doorway of my room at the Sportsman's Country Club.

Quickly, Petacque asked me if I would plead for my brother James Earl Ray to give himself up. I responded with, "I was pleading for him not to give himself up." I then slammed the door in Petacque's face!

In the next day's edition of the *Chicago Sun Times*, there was a long story by Art Petacque, accompanied by an unflattering photo of me standing in the doorway in my underwear. The headline read something like, Jerry Ray pleads for his brother to give himself up in the assassination of Martin Luther King. Petacque's story was completely opposite what I had told him. It was an outright lie. To counteract Petacque's bullshit story, I contacted the *Chicago Daily News* and told them I would give them an in-depth interview if they would send me an honest reporter who would write down exactly what I said. They sent me a reporter named Jerry Lipson. I gave Lipson my version of what had gone down with Petacque and me – the truth. The *Chicago Daily News* ran it exactly as I told it to Lipson.

Not too long ago, I read that Petacque was in the Chicago Journalism Hall of Fame. That's a joke because I don't see how he kept from ending up in the trunk of some Cadillac parked at O'Hare Airport – since he was a big time mob reporter. Looking back on it, though, I think he may have been working with the FBI – as one of their "friendly reporters," and they may have protected him. Also, I believe that the FBI gave Petacque that badge and told him where he could find me.

The biggest magazines in 1968 were *Life*, *Look* and the *Saturday Evening Post*. The cover story for the May 3, 1968 edition of *Life* magazine was titled, "The Accused Killer RAY alias

GALT, The Revealing Story of a Mean Kid." It pictured a black and white group photo of Ewing School Class of 1938. Naturally, the reader's eye goes directly to the center of the photo, straight to a seemingly unhappy, mean-looking kid dressed in overalls. However, as my brother later pointed out in his book, that kid was not Jimmy; he was Jimmy's classmate and boyhood friend, Robey Peacock. Ten year-old Jimmy is underneath the small red arrow, to the right of Robey – second row, right-hand side. This is just another example of how the media was going to any length to trick and convince the public that James Earl Ray was the "lone nut" assassin of Martin Luther King – regardless of the truth.

***

I continued working at the Sportsman's Country Club. The management at the Sportsman's even rented me a room in nearby Lake Forest, so I could have some peace when I was off work. However, I could tell there was a strain building between my employers and me. After Art Petacque's story in the *Chicago Sun Times*, a horde of local police, FBI and media reporters camped out every day at the Sportsman's wanting to talk to me. Even though I had been a good employee, I knew it was only a matter of time before they had to let me go. They were receiving a great deal of negative publicity by keeping me there. Plus, it was becoming an unavoidable distraction to the other employees.

On June 8, 1968, a news bulletin announced that Scotland Yard detectives at London's Heathrow Airport had captured James Earl Ray. I saw it on the news. That day, June 8, 1968, was the last day I worked at the Sportsman's Country Club. I turned in my time, packed my things, collected my last check and headed for St. Louis. When I arrived in St. Louis, I helped my brother John run the Grapevine Tavern.

As I mentioned, the Grapevine Tavern was quite a wild joint. We were supposed to close the Grapevine at midnight, but the cops allowed us to stay open as late as we wanted. We had pool cue fights over bets on pool games, and a guy who'd done time with John would dance naked on the table to Jim Ed Brown's "Pop a Top" on the jukebox.

At the Grapevine, we had two female bartenders, one for day shift, which John oversaw, and one for evening shift, which I oversaw. John demanded a certain degree of respect from those who patronized the Grapevine. It was imperative that customers addressed John as either "Mr. Ray" or "The Commander." Failure to do so could result in John's right fist up against a jaw – and John had a punch like a champion boxer. I once saw him hit a man close to 250 pounds – the same guy who danced naked on the table – and knock him flat on his back. I stayed with John at the Grapevine off and on for about two years. The reason I eventually got out was that I was helping Jimmy, and also I knew if I didn't get out, I'd end up either killing someone or getting killed myself because of the kind of people who showed up there.

\*\*\*

After Jimmy was captured at Heathrow Airport, he became headline news in just about every newspaper, almost every day. Originally, he was held at Brixton Prison in England, but at the request of someone from the U.S. Attorney General's Office, he was transferred to and held at Wadsworth Prison, a more secure facility than Brixton. I didn't know it at the time – he later told me – but Jimmy initially contacted F. Lee Bailey, one of the more prominent attorneys in the United States at that time, to represent him. Bailey wrote back to Jimmy and said he couldn't represent him because of Bailey's close relationship with the King family. Jimmy finally was able to make contact with and retain Attorney Arthur Hanes Sr., out of Birmingham, Alabama. Hanes flew to England and visited Jimmy in jail. Hanes was well known, and Jimmy knew about him from having read about some of his cases in the past. Actually,

Jimmy retained both Arthur Hanes Sr. and Arthur Hanes Jr. a father and son attorney team.

Before Jimmy was extradited back to the United States, and before we knew that he had retained the two attorneys, John and I attempted to set up a legal fund for Jimmy. We intended to rent a P.O. box at the Memphis Post Office, which would be mentioned along with any stories run about Jimmy in the *Chicago Daily News*. The newspaper would run an ad about our P.O. box in Memphis, to which funds could be contributed to the defense of James Earl Ray.

John and I traveled to Memphis to set up that plan. The evening we arrived, John was tired and wanted to sleep, but I went down the street to a tavern within walking distance of our motel room. After I finished my last beer, I walked outside, and there sat a Memphis Police squad car. An officer got out and ordered me to get in the backseat of the squad car. Realizing I didn't have much of a choice, I complied. They took me to police headquarters in downtown Memphis where they took all of my personal belongings – including my billfold, which had some important addresses and telephone numbers. I spent the night in the Memphis jail. The next morning the police came and got me and heavily questioned me about all the names, addresses and telephone numbers in my billfold. They'd contacted John while I was locked up and they released me at the front desk where John was waiting for me.

Meanwhile, a Memphis newspaper ran a story saying that the brother of James Earl Ray had been arrested and jailed for causing a disturbance at a tavern in downtown Memphis. That evening a crew from the local news station went to the tavern to interview the bartender. It aired on television. The bartender told the news crew that he had served me a couple beers, and that I had not caused any disturbance, whatsoever. In fact, no one in the tavern that night knew who I was. I'd just sipped my beer and had not conversed with anyone.

This is merely another example of the many ways the media attempted to portray the Ray family as beer-guzzling thugs and troublemakers. After the incident in Memphis, when the police kept me in jail overnight and the news said that I'd started trouble in the bar, John and I gave up on the idea of contributions to Jimmy's defense being made to the P.O. box at the Memphis Post Office.

*** 

Jimmy's extradition from England back to the United States became very complicated. The U.S. Attorney General's Office filed its extradition request to British authorities based on the word of one so-called witness, Charles Quitman Stephens. At first, British authorities balked and refused to send Jimmy back, but they finally relented to pressure from the United States.

To illuminate the specious nature of the so-called evidence or testimony on which the extradition was based, it is necessary to describe Charlie Stephens and his common-law wife, Grace Stephens. The Stephens were renting room #6B of Bessie Brewer's flophouse in Memphis, Tennessee at the time of the King assassination, and at the same time my brother Jimmy rented room #5B at Bessie's.

On April 4, 1968, the day of the King assassination, Jimmy used the alias John Willard to rent #5B at Bessie's. Until the day he died, Jimmy said he was following the instructions of a smuggler named Raoul – the same Raoul he told me about at the Chicago Train Station – when he rented room #5B that day. Charlie and Grace lived in room #6B, right next to #5B.

Charlie Stephens was a known drunk with a lengthy police record for public intoxication. Right after King died, the authorities had posted a $100,000.00 reward for information leading to the arrest and conviction of King's assassin. Charlie Stephens claimed to the investigators that he saw my brother, James Earl Ray, carrying a green bundle, and walking down the hallway of Bessie Brewer's flophouse immediately after King was shot.

Astonishingly, Grace Stephens adamantly refuted what her husband Charlie was saying. She was claiming that Charlie didn't see anyone walking down the hallway after King was shot because Charlie was splayed across their bed, passed-out drunk! Some of this information was reported on the television news. I got most of my news from TV back then and a little on radio. [Later, during 1978-1979, I met with Grace Stephens and we had several lengthy conversations about what had happened. She repeated some of the news reports I had heard before and provided additional information and details.]

A Yellow Cab driver named James McGraw testified that just minutes before King was shot, he had gone up to the Stephens' room to give Charlie a taxi ride, but Charlie had been too drunk to transport.

Further, Wayne Chastain, then a reporter for the *Memphis Press Scimitar* newspaper (no longer in existence), talked to Stephens shortly after King was shot. Chastain told me, personally, that Charlie Stephens was "drunk on his ass!"

Even Memphis Police Captain Tommy Smith testified that he spoke with Stephens just minutes after King was shot, and that Charlie had been "too intoxicated to carry on an intelligent conversation."

Nevertheless, on July 19, 1968, a U.S. Air Force jet flew Jimmy from England to Memphis, Tennessee to stand trial in the murder of Reverend Dr. Martin Luther King, Jr.

I still remember that newspaper photo of the Shelby County sheriff escorting Jimmy to the Shelby County Jail. My brother Jimmy was wearing glasses, some kind of jumpsuit, his hands cuffed in front of him and his head lowered.

Before they extradited Jimmy back to the United States, however, something very disturbing transpired. The general consensus among most observers – judges, prosecutors, defense attorneys, writers, family members, the interested public – was that Jimmy would go to trial, take the witness stand, and testify in his own defense, denying the allegations. The .30.06 Remington rifle that had been found in the doorway of Canipe's Amusements, wrapped in the green bundle next door to the stairwell leading up to Bessie Brewer's flophouse, supposedly had Jimmy's fingerprints on it. Jimmy admitted purchasing that rifle under the alias Harvey Lowmeyer at Aeromarine Supply Company on March 30, 1968.

There are two, conflicting, explanations for this. The "official" explanation is that James Earl Ray dropped it during his flight from the rooming house following the shooting of Dr. King. The HSCA said Ray came out with the bundle intending to put it in his car trunk and saw police rounding the Firehouse and dropped it in a panic inside the doorway to Canipe's Amusements to conceal it, which is where they found it. Ray then allegedly drove off in his white Mustang at high speed.

The other explanation is that it was planted there to frame Ray for the murder, perhaps by Raoul or others. Guy Canipe himself said he saw the bundle dropped there by a man five minutes before he heard the rifle shot. While some items in the bundle clearly belonged to James Earl Ray, others did not, including underwear (with a laundry tag attached) that would not have fit him. Some items had his fingerprints on them; others did not. His prison radio was in the bundle, with his inmate number from the last place he escaped from, but Ray said he did not take it with him when he left. Ray purchased the Remington rifle .30.06 on instructions from Raoul, he said, having to exchange a rifle he had bought for that one. The owner of the gun shop where it was purchased said the only person he had ever met with less knowledge about rifles than Ray was the HSCA investigator who came to ask him about it. The FBI did not test the rifle that day to see if it had been fired. A subsequent independent test by Judge Joe Brown found that the rifle was not conclusively matched to the bullet. When he asked for the FBI and HSCA ballistics test results, and requested that the rifle be cleaned for a confirming second test, Judge Brown was denied and then pulled off the case by the Tennessee Supreme Court as "biased" in favor of Ray. The rifle remains untested. It is now housed at the National Civil

Rights Museum in Memphis. There are many indications in the hard evidence that Ray was not the assassin and that the fatal shot could not have come from the rooming house bathroom window. This bundle of incriminating evidence seems to have been planted in the doorway by others who were setting Ray up to take the blame.

When the rifle was found in the doorway of Canipe's Amusements, it was immediately sent off to FBI headquarters in Washington, D.C. to be tested, along with the fatal slug extracted from King's corpse. On April 15, 1968, Special Agent Robert Frazier conducted a ballistics test on that rifle. After comparing it to the bullets fired through it, Special Agent Frazier could not conclude the slug that killed King was fired from the rifle in question.[1]

So, at that point, the only so-called evidence the prosecution/state had against Jimmy was the statement of drunken Charles Quitman Stephens – whose own wife, Grace Stephens, was adamantly refuting his statement, further weakening the state's case against Jimmy. Authorities and investigators were keeping close tabs on the Stephens because they played such a vital role in the case. Mr. and Mrs. Stephens were poor and without a vehicle. The Memphis Police were escorting them around Memphis at their request. At some point in July 1968, the Memphis Police drove Charlie and Grace Stephens to John Gaston Hospital in Memphis so Grace could have a leg injury looked at. According to a TV news story at the time, while Grace Stephens was having her leg tended to, a psychiatrist, completely unannounced, appeared on the scene and informed her that her true problems were of a mental nature.

Against her will, Grace was then taken and confined to John Gaston Hospital's psychiatric ward, where she was forced to undergo a battery of psychological tests. On July 31, 1968, Grace Stephens was taken before Memphis Probate Judge Harry Pierotti. Judge Pierotti declared her mentally incompetent and had her committed to nearby Western State Psychi-

---

1      Special Agent Frazier also conducted the ballistics testing on the Mannilicher-Carcano rifle that Lee Harvey Oswald allegedly used to shoot President John F. Kennedy on November 22, 1963, in Dallas, Texas. John Armstrong, *Harvey & Lee: How the CIA Framed Oswald*. (Arlington, Texas: Quasar, 2003), 510-511.

atric Hospital in Bolivar, Tennessee. Once a person is declared mentally incompetent, or insane, his/her testimony is virtually useless in court. Grace Stephens' rebuttal of the state's only eyewitness, her husband, had been neutralized.

Grace Stephens remained a ward of Western State Psychiatric Hospital for about ten years, until around 1977 or 1978, when Attorney Mark Lane took over as Jimmy's lead defense counsel. When Lane took the helm, he systematically identified and located all relevant witnesses to question. Mark Lane was able to track down Grace at Western State.

Lane finally got Grace released from psychiatric incarceration, but he had a difficult time doing so because the state's authorities blocked him at every turn. The reason is rather obvious: they wanted to keep Grace Stephens hushed. To secure Grace Stephens' release, Lane had to get the help of Reverend James Lawson – the black minister who had asked King to come down to Memphis to lead the garbage workers' march. Had it not been for Lawson, I doubt she ever would have been released. In fact, since she had no family to speak of, once she was released from Western State, she lived with Attorney Mark Lane for a while. Lane moved to Memphis so he could devote himself full time to defending Jimmy.

I personally talked to Grace Stephens. She appeared to be in excellent mental health. Grace told me:

> Jerry, I stayed locked up all those years because I wouldn't go along with what the prosecution and state wanted. I saw a man walking down the hallway after King was shot, and I said back then that it wasn't your brother, and I say to this day that it wasn't your brother. I saw a Mexican-looking guy walking down the hallway after King got shot, and Charlie never saw anybody.

The state never paid Charlie Stephens his $100,000.00 reward. After he realized he'd been bamboozled, Charlie confessed, live, to Dan Rather that everything he'd sworn about seeing Jimmy walking down the hallway of Bessie Brewer's had been a lie. I've got a cassette tape of it. However, it didn't do any good because the state had their man – James Earl Ray, a white, 40 year old career criminal and fugitive from justice. The naïve public bought it. From what I hear, Charlie Stephens died, broke, out on the streets.

***

A special jail cell was constructed in Memphis for Jimmy. What they did, actually, was knock out a wall dividing two cells and turned them into one big cell. Then they reconfigured the cell to confine him in conditions that were atrocious. They placed steel plates over the windows. Bright lights were on him 24 hours a day. And when I say bright lights, I mean intense, glaring, studio lights that nearly blinded you. When entering the cell, everyone – attorneys, deputies, whoever – would instantly bring up a hand across his eyes to shield them from these lights. Jimmy couldn't use the restroom in privacy. Deputies were always in the cell with him. When he would meet with his attorney – Arthur Hanes Sr. and Jr. at first, and later, Percy Foreman – they would have to lie on the floor and whisper in each other's ear because they knew everything was being monitored.

Attorney Mark Lane later said that the prisoners of the Nuremburg World War II trials were jailed under better conditions than James Earl Ray. It was an obvious attempt by the System to break down Jimmy emotionally, physically and mentally, in hopes of rendering him incapable of making sound decisions.

After Jimmy was brought back to Memphis, I would drive up from St. Louis to visit him about every other weekend and assist him as best I could in preparing his defense. It was tough seeing Jimmy jailed under those conditions … and not being able to do anything about it.

***

At that time, 1968, one of the most prominent journalists in America was a man named William Bradford Huie. Like the Haneses, Huie was from Alabama – Hartselle, Alabama, to be exact. Not only did Huie regularly write articles for Life, Look and Post magazines, he also had some best-selling books. I can think of three of his books that were made into movies, *The Klansman, Mississippi Burning* and *The Execution of Private Slovik*. Of course, Huie was interested in writing about James Earl Ray and the Reverend Dr. Martin Luther King, Jr. assassination because at the time it was the biggest story in the country.

As I said earlier, Jimmy had initially contacted attorney F. Lee Bailey. When Bailey said he could not take the case because of his relationship with the King family, Jimmy contacted the Haneses, and they agreed to represent him. When Huie found out that Hanes Sr. and Jr. were representing Jimmy, Huie contacted them and told them that he was interested in collaborating with them if he could get exclusive rights to Jimmy's story.

At first, Huie said that he was of the opinion that a conspiracy was likely in the MLK assassination, and that, very possibly, Jimmy was not the gunman. In July 1968, before my brother Jimmy had been extradited back to the United States, Attorney Arthur Hanes Sr. had traveled to Britain to talk to Jimmy. At that time, Jimmy signed a contract with Arthur Hanes Sr., giving the Haneses power of attorney to act in Jimmy's behalf – which included a three-way writing deal with Huie. The three-way deal stipulated that Jimmy, the Haneses, and Huie would each receive one-third from all profits resulting from any related works about Jimmy's case that Huie wrote and sold.

Aware that I was particularly close to Jimmy, Huie sent me a first-class round-trip ticket from St. Louis to Huntsville, Alabama. On November 1, 1968, I flew to Huntsville and as I stepped off the plane, there stood William Bradford Huie with a quart of Jack Daniel's Whiskey in hand – Black Label, to be precise! Even though I generally didn't drink hard liquor – still don't – I accepted the bottle of Tennessee's finest. But it made me wonder if William Bradford Huie thought that all of us in the Ray family were so dense and shallow he could buy us for a bottle of whiskey.

Huie had already rented me a room at the Airport Hotel and we went there to talk. Huie wasted little time. He got right down to business. He stated he was ready to write a book about the King assassination and Jimmy's involvement. He said he was convinced that Jimmy did not fire the fatal shot. He also told me that he had signed an agreement with the Haneses. This agreement specified how the legal fees for the Haneses, in their representation of Jimmy, would come from sales generated by Huie's book, as well as related articles. He stated that his book, no doubt, would be a bestseller, a claim reinforced by Huie's past literary accomplishments. He also said his book would depict Jimmy in the role of a patsy rather than as the shooter, which appeared to be Huie's true stance.

However, for all his supposed good will toward Jimmy and me, Huie wanted something in return. He wanted me to convince Jimmy not to take the witness stand at his trial because, so he said, his book would be worth more if my brother didn't testify. If Jimmy did testify, then his information would be public knowledge, accessible to all; but if Jimmy didn't testify, and instead made such information available to Huie and the book, it would be accessible only by way of the book.

And … Huie offered me a substantial incentive. He told me he would give me $13,000.00 up front if I could get Jimmy to guarantee that he would not take the witness stand on his own behalf. The reason for the figure of $13,000.00 was that was how much money Jimmy had already made for Huie, thus far, as payment for articles Huie had written about the King assassination and sold to a number of magazines.

Moreover, on top of this, when Jimmy was brought back to Memphis, Arthur Hanes Sr. had visited him in his jail cell and had my brother sign a new contract whereby the Haneses would get their third plus Jimmy's third until the Haneses had accumulated a certain amount of money as legal fees –

somewhere in the $200,000.00 range, I'm pretty sure. Huie had copies of both contracts – the one Jimmy had signed with the Haneses in England and the new one signed in Memphis. Huie informed me that he wanted the contract to go back to the way it was originally, where he, the Haneses and Jimmy, each, received one-third of the profits. He said that I needed money, and Jimmy would have a better attitude if he were receiving some money.

I realized that Huie didn't give a damn about Jimmy or me, and that he was using money to manipulate the situation and have his way.

Huie went on to say that the $13,000.00 was just "starters," that there would be "plenty more" if I could convince Jimmy not to take the witness stand. From that meeting with Huie at the Airport Hotel, November 1, 1968, one moment particularly stands out. After Huie offered the $13,000.00, I countered that possibly the Haneses might not go for that. Immediately, Huie's ego overtook him, and he puffed up like a spoiled kid. "I'm the one controlling the money, here!" he stormed. "You let me worry about the Haneses; they'll do whatever I tell them to do!"

Huie's words and behavior convinced me that he, not the Haneses, was controlling the case. I told Huie that I would relay to Jimmy what he had said. Huie left the room. I spent the night, November 1, 1968, inside my room at the Airport Hotel and flew back to St. Louis the next day, November 2, 1968.

Within a week or so, the next time Jimmy was allowed to have visitors, I drove from St. Louis to Memphis and paid my brother a visit. I told Jimmy what had happened with Huie, and that he should let the Haneses go and hire another attorney. "Huie's controlling the case, not the Haneses," I said to Jimmy. At this point, neither I nor anyone in the family had said anything to Jimmy about attorneys or about what should be done in preparing for the trial because we knew that Jimmy had a mind of his own. After meeting with Huie in Alabama, however, I was convinced that I would have to be Jimmy's ears and eyes on the outside if there was to be any hope of him

receiving a fair shake concerning his alleged role in the assassination of Martin Luther King.

Jimmy's trial was scheduled to take place in just a couple of
weeks, so we had to take action quickly. Jimmy agreed with me
about Huie and the Haneses, and told me to contact a lawyer
over in Mississippi – just across the state line from Memphis. I
can't remember the Mississippi lawyer's name, but he was well
known, and Jimmy had read quite a bit about him. I contacted the Mississippi lawyer about taking my brother's case. He
told me he would have to have some money up front. Neither
Jimmy or I, nor anyone in our family, had any money, so we
quickly nixed that idea.

Next, I immediately contacted Attorney Richard J. Ryan out of
Memphis. Right off, Ryan expressed an interest in representing
Jimmy, but he also said that my brother's case was of too great
a magnitude for him to take on as the primary defense counsel.
He went on to say, though, that he would be glad to assist the
Haneses. The problem was that although we were about to get rid
of the Haneses, but we weren't ready to broadcast it to the public.
The next time I visited Jimmy, I told him what had transpired
with Ryan and the Mississippi lawyer. I then told my brother that
maybe he should consider contacting Attorney Percy Foreman,
known as the "Texas Tiger," who practiced out of Houston, Texas.

I had once read that Foreman had defended somewhere
around 900 accused murderers. All of them had been acquitted, except for one, who'd been executed, and fifty or so who'd
been sent to prison. I researched some of his cases and knew
enough to have confidence in Foreman's skills. Even though
Jimmy was still intent on finding a Tennessee-based attorney,
I went ahead on my own and contacted Percy Foreman. [2] It

---

2          Years later, Percy Foreman represented Charles Harrelson, the father of actor Woody Harrelson. Convicted of killing Federal Judge John Ward, Charles Harrelson is
currently serving a life sentence in a Federal penitentiary. While in custody, he admitted
involvement in the assassination of President John F. Kennedy, November 22, 1963, in Dallas, Texas. However, Foreman did not represent Harrelson on the murder of the judge, but
on another case. Interestingly, Percy Foreman, for a short period, served as an attorney for
Jack Ruby, the convicted murder of Lee Harvey Oswald, JFK's alleged assassin. Armstrong,
Harvey & Lee, 551; Robert Neiman, "Captain Jack Dean, United States Marshall, 20th Century Shining Star," *The Texas Ranger Dispatch*, Winter 2003.

just so happened that when I called Foreman the first time, by a stroke of luck he happened to be in his office and picked up the telephone himself. At first, Foreman said that even though he was interested in representing my brother, Jimmy needed to send him a letter requesting that he visit him in jail. I went back and told Jimmy what Foreman had said. Jimmy still was intent on finding a Tennessee-based attorney who was familiar with Tennessee courts and laws. For a week or better, I kept trying to find a Tennessee attorney – but no luck. By then Jimmy's trial was only a few days away, so I decided to contact Percy Foreman again.

Miraculously enough – once again – Foreman answered his office telephone when I called the second time. Foreman still wanted the letter from Jimmy requesting that he visit him in jail. However, when I informed Foreman that Jimmy's trial was to take place in only a few days, and that time would not permit such an exchange of letters, Foreman agreed to hop on a plane and come to Memphis to talk with Jimmy. Normally, an attorney of Foreman's caliber wouldn't even have considered taking a murder case on such short notice. However, since the James Earl Ray case was proving to be one of the biggest cases of all time, I felt that Foreman would want to be part of Jimmy's defense, one way or the other. My hunch proved correct.

My brother John traveled to Memphis with me on this visit to Jimmy. The next day, John and I picked up Percy Foreman at the Memphis International Airport. We then drove him to see Jimmy in his jail cell. After they talked for a considerable amount of time, Foreman left Jimmy's cell and held a press conference – announcing that he was taking over as lead defense counsel. By that time, the Haneses, in preparation for Jimmy's trial, which was to begin in just a couple days, had set up headquarters at a hotel in Memphis. As expected, they were disappointed and upset at getting dismissed by Jimmy.

Foreman flew back to Texas to collect legal and personal items he would need, and then flew back to Memphis in just a few days. When he returned, he set up headquarters in the historic Peabody Hotel, located in downtown Memphis. On my next trip to Memphis to visit Jimmy, Foreman summonsed me to his room at the Peabody. When I arrived at his room, Foreman greeted me dressed in a T-shirt, boxer shorts and dress socks. First, he handed me some money and told me to go down to the liquor store and get him a bottle of scotch. I returned with a bottle of scotch and soda water. I poured him about a three-finger shot and he looked at me as though I'd lost my mind. "Pour me a damn drink! And don't mess it up with that soda water, neither," he ordered. I filled up the glass, gave it to him straight, and he turned it up and killed it off. After about three more rounds, which had the bottle way below half full, the "Texas Tiger" show began.

Percy Foreman was a great big, tall man, about 6'4", 250 pounds. He told me that when he was a young man he had wanted to be a professional wrestler. In fact, he might have wrestled either in high school or college – I'm not sure. And as large as he was in physical stature, he was even larger in personal ego. You couldn't get a word in edgewise with Foreman, because he manipulated the entire conversation by loudly revealing his accomplishments. I have to admit, though, that he was a great showman. That night he told me that laws weren't worth the paper they were written on. "If a lawyer isn't a good actor, he won't be successful," he bellowed.

He would knock back a healthy slug of scotch and prance around the room like a rooster. He really enjoyed rehashing the Candace Mossler murder trial in which he had defended Candy Mossler. He said, "Everybody knew that Candy and her stud nephew cold-bloodedly murdered Jacques Mossler for his money. I also knew, however, that Jacques had participated in some of Candy's sexcapades, and that's what I built my case on. When I addressed the jury, I portrayed Jacques Mossler as a wealthy banker and sex degenerate who'd swept naive Candy – who in reality was nothing but a money hungry, sex-starved, self-serving vixen – off her feet with his money and forced her into those sexual trysts because of his frustrating impotency, thus turning a good girl into a bad girl. By the time I was through with the jury, they wanted to raise Jacques Mossier from the grave and kill him all over again!

"And I can do the same damn thing with your brother's case. Hell, boy, they don't have any solid evidence on your brother, only the word of a known drunk and fingerprints on a weapon that they can't ballistically match to the slug that killed King. This is the easiest murder case I've ever defended; my granddaughter could beat it; I don't even have to prepare. All I've got to do is sit here in the Peabody, call room service, sip on good scotch, and give some interviews to the press until the trial."

I left Foreman's room that night convinced that he could do just that, get Jimmy an acquittal because, as Foreman said, the prosecution didn't have any solid evidence on Jimmy, as far as I could tell. I told Jimmy what Foreman had told me at the Peabody. He was glad to hear the news. Even drained and down as he was, given the horrendous conditions he'd been jailed under, I could tell that the news of what Foreman had told me lifted my brother's spirits tremendously. I left Jimmy feeling good.

Foreman maintained his confident stance of being able to get Jimmy acquitted until around January or February of 1969. Without warning, he suddenly underwent what I call a "legal metamorphosis." Foreman changed faces completely. He went to Jimmy and told him that if he insisted on going to trial and taking the stand, more than likely, he would get the death penalty, especially given King's public image and status. Foreman even traveled to St. Louis and visited with our dad and other family members – crying and putting on a show – trying to convince us to convince Jimmy to enter a guilty plea. He told us that if Jimmy demanded a trial and took the witness stand, he surely would fry in the hot seat. Foreman also said that authorities were looking into the criminal history of our family. He claimed they knew that our dad was a parole violator from way back and could put him back in prison – even though Dad posed no threat and his case dated

back to the late twenties. Also, Foreman told me word was
circulating that if there was any substance whatsoever to Jimmy's tale of a man named Raoul, then it merely was a cover
name for me, and I probably was involved in the King assassination – maybe even the shooter. I remember thinking,
Uh-oh, King was killed on a Thursday, and Thursday was my
day off at the Sportsman's. I can see how this is taking shape
… and it's not good.

When Jimmy became aware of Foreman's drastic switch in
legal strategy, he wanted to fire him. In fact, a few weeks before
the trial, John visited our brother Jimmy in his Memphis jail
cell. During that visit, Jimmy told John that he was considering firing Foreman and not entering a guilty plea. Even though
that conversation was supposed to be private, it was picked up
by microphones throughout Jimmy's cell. The deputies listening in passed the information on to the media.

When Judge Preston Battle heard that Jimmy was considering firing Foreman, and not entering a guilty plea, he said that
he would not allow any further continuances, and if Jimmy
fired Foreman, he would have to go to trial with a public defender. Well, we figured a public defender would be severely
manipulated by the Memphis District Attorney's Office. As a
result of Judge Battle's decision, we didn't have much choice
other than to keep Percy Foreman.

On March 9, 1969, Percy Foreman visited Jimmy inside his
jail cell. My brother later told me that Foreman was "tore all to
pieces" about him possibly not entering the guilty plea. Jimmy
also said that, during that March 9, 1969 meeting, Foreman
took on a much more sinister disposition. He informed Jimmy
that not entering a guilty plea would make Foreman look bad,
and if Jimmy did that, then Foreman, basically, would do nothing to defend him. Foreman made it blatantly clear to Jimmy
that his refusal to enter a guilty plea could result in prison for
me and for our dad. I believe it may serve a useful purpose to
take a look at the whys of Percy Foreman drastically switching
stances in his defense of Jimmy.

Foreman was known to be a man of exceptional legal, social, financial and political means. It was known that he had close ties to a variety of powerful people – legislators on Capitol Hill in Washington, D.C., the billionaire Hunt brothers out of Dallas, Texas, the Murchison family who owned the Dallas Cowboys professional football team, FBI Director J. Edgar Hoover, Teamster legend Jimmy Hoffa and New Orleans mafia boss Carlos Marcello.

Rumor had it that Frank Liberto was a key player in the King assassination. At the time of King's death, Liberto owned and operated LL&L – Liberto, Liberto & Latch, a food produce company in Memphis. In addition to being in the produce business, Liberto was a major crime figure in Memphis. Liberto had grown up in New Orleans, supposedly was a close childhood friend of Carlos Marcello, and was his representative in Memphis.

Also living in Memphis at the time of the King assassination was a man named Loyd Jowers who was then in his forties. Jowers, something of a man about town, owned and operated Jim's Grill, located on South Main Street in Memphis, directly across from the Lorraine Motel where King was standing when he was killed. Directly above Jim's Grill was Bessie Brewer's flophouse. Jimmy admitted renting room #5B from Bessie Brewer on the day of the King assassination. Jimmy also claimed, and maintained until his death, that he met with Raoul inside room #5B on the afternoon of April 4, 1968.

As mentioned earlier, the prosecution argued that Jimmy shot King from the commonly shared bathroom of Bessie Brewer's flophouse – just down the hallway from room #5B. Records confirm that Jimmy was at the New Rebel Hotel the day before, on April 3, 1968 where, according to Jimmy, he had handed over the alleged murder rifle to Raoul on that date, April 3, 1968. Jimmy said that, having given Raoul the rifle at the New Rebel Hotel in Memphis on April 3, he – Jimmy – never saw the rifle again. In addition, my brother claimed – and maintained up until his death – that he was not even in the vicinity of Bessie Brewer's flophouse or the Lorraine Motel at the time of the King murder.

### Enter one Loyd Jowers.

In addition to owning and running Jim's Grill, Jowers also had been a Memphis policeman who had ties to and dealings with the Memphis underworld, specifically Frank Liberto. Jim's Grill was a well-known hangout for both Memphis Police and those who operated on the opposite side of the law. Also, many believed that Jowers was heavily indebted to Liberto over a large gambling bill.

In 1993, Jowers appeared on national television with ABC's Sam Donaldson and claimed that he was "indirectly" involved in the King assassination and wanted to clear the record. Jowers made the following claims to Donaldson, as well as to other sources:

Jowers said that he stashed the actual King murder rifle inside Jim's Grill for a period of time before April 4, 1968.

Jowers said that on the day of the King assassination he gave the actual murder rifle to King's actual killer, a Memphis policeman.

From the row of hedges that lined the rear of Jim's Grill, across the way, some 200 feet from room #306 of the Lorraine Motel, Jowers said he took, hand-to-hand, the actual murder rifle from King's actual killer, and stashed it yet again inside Jim's Grill for an additional period of time.

At this point, it is important to bring in a statement made by an eye witness to the assassination, *New York Times* reporter Earl Caldwell. Writing in a column for the *New York Times*, which ran April 5, 1968, the day after King's death, Caldwell said – and later testified, and continues to swear to this day – that immediately after King was shot, in the row of bushes lining the rear of Jim's Grill, Caldwell observed a "puff of smoke" and "a white man" rise from a "crouched position" and move out through the bushes.

[The official story places Ray in the rooming house at the time, despite evidence to the contrary from Grace Stevens and Ray's own account of changing a tire at a nearby gas station where witnesses saw him. It also contradicts the official version of the source of the shot. Jowers testified that this gunman was not Ray, but someone else who was known to him (Jowers) and that he delivered the gun to the back door of the restaurant following the shooting. Another man, not Ray, picked up the actual rifle used in the murder the next day.]

In November and December 1999, at the Shelby County Court House, Memphis, there was a civil trial involving Loyd Jowers and his testimony about the King assassination. In 1999, Jowers was old and in the frailest of health, suffering terminally from heart and liver ailments. He once again had come forward saying that he wished to clear the record concerning what he knew about the King assassination. Jowers stated that he was ready to identify King's actual killer, who was not James Earl Ray, but rather, a former Memphis policeman.

Jowers wanted immunity from being charged as an accomplice in the murder of Dr. King and conspiracy to kill him. The case was against Loyd Jowers and other unnamed conspirators. It was brought by the family of Dr. King in civil court, for damages in the violation of their civil rights. It was a wrongful death trial, involving a conspiracy. The full transcript can be seen at the website of the King Center in Atlanta.

The King family sued Jowers for a prearranged small compensation (Coretta Scott King called it a "token amount") equal to the amount spent by the sanitation workers union in Memphis, $100.00, which the King family donated to them. Jowers implicated a different gunman, a former policeman and sharpshooter. Jowers said he was asked by conspirators to hire the gunman, the policeman, and that he was paid for the job. The policeman was deceased at the time of the trial. The trial convinced the jury that Ray was innocent of the crime and that there had been a conspiracy to kill King, a conspiracy that reached to the top levels of the US government, involving military intelligence, FBI and others.

At the civil trial, longtime Memphis attorney Lewis Garrison – a highly distinguished and respected man – represented Jowers who was charged with having a role in the conspiracy to kill King. The civil action for wrongful death was brought by the King family, represented by attorney William Pepper, Esq.

Due to his poor health at the time, Jowers never took the stand to testify. He died not too long after the civil trial. It is important that, although the jury found Jowers guilty of a small degree of involvement in the King murder, they found Jimmy innocent of being the triggerman in the King murder.

At the trial, presiding Judge James E. Swearengen stated:

> As I told you, this is a case on conspiracy. Conspiracy I guess in general terms would mean carrying out a design or plan where two or more have agreed to commit an act to do injury or damage. And the planning, of course, is not enough. They have to, in addition to the planning, do an act pursuant to that plan in order to be a co-conspirator.

The jury found that the murder of Martin Luther King, Jr. had been the result of a high level government conspiracy. Mrs. Coretta Scott King, on behalf of her family, stated at the time:

> There is abundant evidence of a major high level conspiracy in the assassination of my husband, Martin Luther King, Jr.… The jury was clearly convinced by the extensive evidence that was presented during the trial that, in addition to Mr. Jowers, the conspiracy of the Mafia, local, state and federal government agencies, were deeply involved in the assassination of my husband. The jury also affirmed overwhelming evidence that identified someone else, not James Earl Ray, as the shooter, and that Mr. Ray was set up to take the blame. [http://www.thekingcenter.org/King-Center/Transcript_trial_info.aspx]

Some alleged that Jowers was merely a self-serving opportunist who had hatched his story about the Memphis police officer being the killer in hopes of securing a lucrative book or movie deal. However, as of November-December 1999, Loyd Jowers was near death – one foot already in the grave – and he was well aware that his time was short. Actually, one of the main reasons he didn't testify in his civil trail was that he was so far along in his illness that he couldn't control bodily functions. But his testimony had been obtained in depositions where he stated that it was Memphis cop who shot King.

As of 1999, the only thing Loyd Jowers stood to gain by telling what he knew in the King assassination was clearing his own conscience and, possibly, clearing the slate with his Maker.

As for Percy Forman, I believe Percy Foreman shifted his position in his defense of Jimmy. King was the victim of a much larger conspiracy. Jimmy was a convenient diversion, his history and profile such that the gullible public would buy into him being the typical "lone nut" assassin. Realizing this, along with the weak, nearly non-existent evidence the state had against Jimmy, Foreman knew he could get my brother an acquittal. I'll always believe that somebody from one of the federal agencies got to Foreman with an ultimatum along these lines: Okay, Mr. Hotshot Attorney, we know you're sharp enough to get Ray acquitted, but we can't allow that because it would cause too much of an uproar and cause us too many headaches. Now, here's the deal – you convince Ray to plead guilty, and we'll keep covering your ass. If you defend Ray and get him acquitted, you're finished! You know we've got a big pile of garbage on you and we can bury you under it.

In the mid 1970s, Percy Foreman was almost disbarred for obstruction of justice for allegedly tampering with a witness in a case involving the billionaire Hunt brothers out of Dallas, Texas. However, Foreman was not disbarred and continued defending high profile cases. Suspiciously, records regarding the behavior that nearly got Foreman disbarred have been lost.

\*\*\*

On March 19, 1969, on Jimmy's 41st birthday, a formal charge was brought against my brother that he had assassinated Dr. King in Memphis, Tennessee on April 4, 1968. The hearing took place in the Shelby County Court House in Memphis. The prosecution team included Memphis District Attorney Phil Canale, Executive Assistant Attorney General Robert K. Dwyer and Assistant Attorney General James C. Beasley. There is no sense in attempting to recall the vast media coverage because just about every media outlet in the country was there that day. Of course, there were the expected writers, too. I distinctly recall well-known writer Clay Blair being present. Blair's book, *The Strange Case of James Earl Ray* was the first to be published about the King assassination.

My brother John and I were the only members of our family present at Jimmy's hearing. Absolutely contrary – a 180-degree spin – to what he had told me at the Peabody Hotel in November 1968, Attorney Percy Foreman, in all his self-serving grandiosity, had Jimmy enter a guilty plea in the assassination of Dr. King. My brother Jimmy agreed to sign a guilty plea, and received a 99 year sentence. It must be remembered that Percy Foreman didn't accept cases where he had to plead a client guilty in a charge of murder. See, it totally went against the grain of his reputation as a successful defender of accused murderers. That should tell you that Foreman's hand was forced in convincing Jimmy to enter a guilty plea.

March 10, 1969, in that Shelby County Court House was the last time I ever saw Jimmy outside a prison setting. After he signed the guilty plea, guards were leading him out, and as they passed by John and me, Jimmy quickly leaned over and whispered in my ear, "Make sure that Foreman gives you the $500.00 so you can go to New Orleans and check out Randy Rosenson." The guard immediately yanked Jimmy away from me and continued leading him out the courtroom. Foreman, John, and I followed them outside the courtroom. They put

Jimmy inside a car. Early the next morning, March 11, 1969, they transported him from Memphis to the main state prison in Nashville, where Jimmy began serving his 99-year sentence.

I'll always regret convincing Jimmy to fire the Haneses and hire Foreman. It's just that what transpired between Huie and me in Huntsville had spooked me about the intentions of the Haneses. Looking in retrospect, I now am convinced that had the Haneses remained as Jimmy's defense counsel, they would have defended him as best they could and very well may have gotten him acquitted. I know that they were prepared to introduce as evidence – exceptionally strong evidence, at that – a statement from Guy Canipe, owner of Canipe's Amusements, the place where the green bundle containing the alleged murder rifle was found. Canipe stated that he heard the bundle being dropped inside the doorway of Canipe's Amusements "ten minutes before King was shot," not after, but before. Arthur Hanes Sr. has passed on, but Arthur Hanes Jr. is still alive.

If I had it to do over, I would have urged Jimmy to keep the Haneses and not have fooled with Percy Foreman. As my brother told me, and many others, Percy Foreman never asked him, "Did you kill Martin Luther King?" Of course, there are a lot of reasons why lawyers, especially criminal lawyers, don't want to ask this question. But Foreman barely asked Jimmy anything about the case and even neglected to work on it, for that matter. He boasted aloud that he didn't need to work on the case because it was an easy win. Foreman took my brother's case for notoriety, book deals, money and his big ego.

The Haneses witnessed the same behavior on the part of Foreman. When Foreman took over the case and was getting Jimmy's files from them, he never asked them that one basic question the whole case pivoted on. Rather, the Haneses said Foreman wanted to talk at length about his legal exploits and drink scotch. Most serious, Foreman told Jimmy to plead guilty, depriving Jimmy right off the bat of his 5th Amendment right not to incriminate himself. What kind of lawyer does that to his client?

***

Those who say that Jimmy admitted to killing King in that Memphis courtroom on March 10, 1969 are incorrect. Jimmy never unequivocally admitted to killing King. Instead, he signed a guilty plea. He entered a plea agreement to avoid threats of the electric chair. Also, you again have to take into consideration the atrocious conditions under which Jimmy was jailed – bright lights on him 24-hours a day; he couldn't perform bodily functions in privacy; everything he said was illegally monitored by hidden microphones, etc. When he allowed Percy Foreman to convince him to plead guilty, Jimmy was suffering from a state of dementia, not in possession of his normal mental faculties.

However, my brother Jimmy did have the mental capacity to convince Percy Foreman to agree to give me $500.00 so I go could go to New Orleans and investigate for Jimmy. After the hearing where Jimmy was forced to cop a guilty plea, John and I accompanied Foreman to his room at the Peabody Hotel. Once we got to the Peabody, Foreman counted out to me $500.000 cash, and then commenced knocking back healthy doses of scotch and bullshitting us in the process about why he'd changed stances in defending our brother. He stated that he wanted John and me to appear with him at a scheduled press conference, to provide support when he told the press his reasons for having Jimmy enter a guilty plea. While John, and I were in Foreman's hotel room, the phone rang. It was Hugh Stanton Jr. the Memphis public defender who'd assisted Foreman in the case. Stanton informed Foreman that Memphis private investigator Renfro Hays, who was hired by Jimmy to do some investigating, claimed he hadn't been paid in full for those services, and was heading to "Union Planters Bank to file an attachment against the $10,000.00 Foreman had received from William Bradford Huie."[3] Even though Foreman was not a young man and was quite large, he raced out of that room in order to block Renfro Hayes from obtaining said monies.

3        Ray, *Tennessee Waltz*, 120.

Foreman held his scheduled press conferences the day of the trial. John and I were there with him. Of course, he lied through his teeth to the press, saying that all along he'd advised James Earl Ray that he couldn't get him acquitted, and that he'd done everything possible in his defense of James Earl Ray, and that, in fact, James Earl Ray should feel fortunate for escaping with a 99-year sentence instead of the electric chair.

I knew Jimmy planned to appeal his case, and, sure enough, he didn't waste any time doing so. In a letter dated March 13, 1969, addressed to Judge Preston Battle, Jimmy wrote that he wished to "inform the honorable court that famous Houston Att. Percy Fourflusher is no longer representing me in any capacity" and "a petition would be filed with the court asking that the guilty plea be set aside, and that any comments by Mr. Foreman to the news media about the King case were not my views but those of the prosecuting attorney, Phil M. Canale."[4] What Jimmy was saying was that Foreman had been on the prosecution's side and not his, which was the truth.

Around this time, mid-March 1969, Jimmy contacted Attorney J.B. Stoner out of Savannah, Georgia. Stoner was well known, although infamously. A self-declared, outspoken racist, Stoner headed the N.S.R.P., National Rights Socialist Party, a Nazi organization so far right and extremist that even the KKK distanced itself. Shortly after Jimmy's extradition from England to Memphis, Stoner had visited him in jail and offered to represent him pro bono. Stoner even told the press that James Earl Ray deserved to win the Congressional Medal of Honor for assassinating Martin Luther King, and that the only thing Stoner had against Adolph Hitler was that he had been too moderate in his treatment of the Jews. When Jimmy had mentioned to the Haneses the possibility of bringing Stoner into the case, the Haneses immediately let my brother know that they would have nothing to do with Stoner, and if Jimmy insisted on bringing in Stoner, the Haneses would resign from the case. Even though Jimmy had refused Stoner initially because of the Haneses, he did allow Stoner to take over

<hr />

4          Ibid., 125.

as lead defense counsel after he officially fired Percy Foreman on March 13, 1969.

[Stoner was, obviously, not a great choice, and Jimmy paid for it over the years, but there were reasons for it, which I will discuss later.]

In addition, we brought two other attorneys in to assist Stoner: Robert Hill, out of Chattanooga, and Attorney Richard Ryan, out of Memphis. The reason for Hill was that Stoner knew him and had a high opinion of him. The reason for Ryan was that he was Memphis-based and a lot of Jimmy's defense would take place in Memphis.

Jimmy sent a second memo to Judge Preston Battle. In a formal petition written in longhand, addressed to Judge Battle, dated March 26, 1969, Jimmy "requested the court to grant [him] a hearing before the expiration of the 30-day time limit governing the filing of a motion for a new trial."[5] Along with the one dated March 13, 1969, this petition to Judge Preston Battle would spark a lot of controversy among legal scholars across the nation – even extending to Capitol Hill in Washington, D.C. The debate concerning the 30-day time limit remains unresolved and continues to this day.

About ten days after Jimmy's trial in Memphis, March 10, 1969, I used the $500.00 Foreman had given me to fly to New Orleans to conduct some research on a man named Randy Rosenson. When I'd visited Jimmy in his Memphis jail cell, as he awaited trial, he had slipped me a note, asking me to check this man out. "Randy Rosenson" was the name Jimmy had whispered in my ear as he walked out of the courtroom after his coerced guilty plea.

Jimmy's note had said that once, when he and Raoul were traveling in New Orleans, Jimmy had discovered a card with the name Randy Rosenson on it. On the back of the card was a telephone number for the Le Bunny Lounge on Canal Street in New Orleans. (Jimmy had almost a photographic memory and had stored all this data in his mind.) The note further indicated that Jimmy and Raoul had met at Le Bunny Lounge

5     Ibid., 126.

on several occasions but, Jimmy said he had never had met anyone named Randy Rosenson.

After I arrived in New Orleans and settled into my hotel room, I hailed a cab for "Le Bunny Lounge on Canal Street." The driver nodded and said, "Yeah, I know where it's at. I'm pretty sure it's one of Carlos Marcello's joints."

At the time, Carlos Marcello was the biggest crime boss in the United States, his criminal empire claiming the entire Gulf region, even stretching into parts of the Caribbean. At the time, there was strong evidence that Marcello, who harbored a bitter hatred for Robert F. Kennedy and John F. Kennedy, had played a direct role in JFK's assassination. Jimmy and Raoul meeting at Le Bunny Lounge, owned by a New Orleans crime boss, an acquaintance of Percy Foreman, an attorney with ties to both the Kennedy assassination and the King assassination – the pieces were coming together, and a big picture was starting to take shape. It was not a pretty picture.

I walked inside, sat down at the bar and ordered a beer. To my surprise, Le Bunny Lounge was an average place. There were only a few other customers there, and they were sitting at tables away from the bar. The cocktail waitress was an attractive woman. We started talking back and forth. I asked her if she knew Randy Rosenson. She stared my way and said, "Who's asking?" I didn't beat around the bush, and replied, "Twenty Dollar Bill, that's who." Needless to say, that got her attention because twenty dollars was a lot of money in those days. As she walked over to me, I pulled a twenty out of my pocket and slid it into her hand.

"I know a Randolph Rosenson," she said. "He comes in here quite often and meets with this Latin-looking guy. He spends money and is a good tipper. He's not from here, though. He told me he is from somewhere in Florida." I then described Jimmy and asked her if she'd ever seen someone of that description with the Latin-looking guy. "Yeah, I remember someone of that description being in here with the Latin-looking guy more than once, but it was a few months back

– Latin guy always picked up the tab. However, even though I've seen the Latin guy with both Rosenson and a man of the description you gave, it was on separate occasions. I've never seen the three in here together. Either it was the Latin guy and Randy – that's what I called Randolph Rosenson – or it was the Latin guy and a dude who fits the description you gave me, never the three together." She also told me that she hadn't seen him around for a while. I threw a couple more beers down the ol' hatch, had the barmaid call me a cab, and I went back to my hotel room.

Unfortunately, I did not locate Rosenson on my trip to New Orleans in 1969. But I kept searching for him for a few years and in 1974, I tracked down a Randy Rosenson in Miami, Florida. I took his picture and I showed it to Jimmy. My brother said this was the Rosenson he had met, but he did not know if he played a role in the assassination or not.

Before I went to New Orleans in March 1969, though, I had made contact with a guy named Kent Courtney. Courtney published a conservative newspaper out of New Orleans – I don't recall the name of it – that the politically liberal considered very far right and extremist. [*Free Men Speak* newspaper, which was renamed the *Independent American*] Courtney and I agreed to meet at a certain park in New Orleans. We met there the day after I visited Le Bunny Lounge. Courtney was waiting for me when I arrived at the park, and I immediately sensed he was a bit uncomfortable. I explained to him that Jimmy had officially fired Foreman, and that J.B. Stoner currently was his lead defense counsel. However, since Stoner was such an avowed racist, Jimmy was concerned that maintaining Stoner as an attorney would go against him, especially since the prosecution and media continued to portray Jimmy as a racist who had killed King because of racial hatred. I told Courtney that Jimmy was in the market for a lead defense counsel, and maybe Courtney, with all his contacts, could point us to someone. Courtney replied that off the top of his head, he couldn't think of anyone, but he would keep us in mind and get back with us. Courtney and I exchanged telephone numbers and shook hands.

By the time I arrived back in St. Louis a few hours later, the story was all over the media about Kent Courtney and me meeting and talking in a park in New Orleans. Come to find out, when Courtney had agreed to talk to me, he had been uneasy about my true intentions and was actually concerned that I might become hostile or that I was trying to set him up. According to the stories, Courtney had called the local police to the park and they had us under surveillance during our meeting, in the event anything violent went down. Of course, there was no violence of any kind.

\*\*\*

As Percy Foreman had told me earlier, word on the street was that either Raoul was a figment of Jimmy's imagination or it was a code name for me. I was certain that Jimmy's Raoul existed in the flesh, at least someone who went by that name, and that he was directly tied to the King assassination. I was certain that my imprisoned brother's future could depend on me locating this man. It was time for the real Raoul to please, stand up.

BEST
IN
DAYTONA
BEACH

J.B. Stoner and Jerry Ray at Daytona Beach in 1969.
Photo courtesy of Jerry Ray.

# CHAPTER FIVE

# STONE COLD STONER

After presiding over the abbreviated "trial" regarding the King assassination, Judge Preston Battle took a vacation and when he returned at the end of March 1969, two letters from Jimmy were waiting on his desk, One letter, dated March 13, 1969, stated that Jimmy had dismissed "Percy Fourflusher" as his legal counsel, and the other, dated March 26, 1969, requested a full-scale trial, as opposed to the hearing where Foreman had hurriedly pushed Jimmy to sign a guilty plea. Judge Battle went into his office to review Jimmy's memos to him. After reviewing Jimmy's petition, realizing that he had fired Percy Foreman and was seeking a trial, Judge Battle instructed assistant prosecutor James Beasley to find out who my brother had in mind for his new defense council. Beasley contacted prison authorities in Nashville, and Jimmy informed them that Attorney Richard Ryan of Memphis would be representing him.

Later in the afternoon of March 31, 1969, Beasley entered Battle's office to deliver the update – only to find Judge Preston Battle dead at his desk, supposedly having died from a heart attack. The Judge's head was slumped over on top of Jimmy's petition, and Jimmy's other letter was in the Judge's desk drawer! There is ample reason to believe that Battle was considering granting Jimmy a new trial. Many link the likelihood of Battle granting Jimmy a new trial with his untimely, eerie death and raise the question of possible foul play.

The rapid sequence of events is startling: Jimmy entered the guilty plea on March 10, 1969; Jimmy wrote to Battle for a change of plea on March 13, 1969; he asked Battle for a full trial on March 26, 1969; and Battle was found dead on March 31, 1969. I'll use these dates as factors in a formula that equates one of the gravest miscarriages of justice in U.S. history. Two Tennessee laws in effect at the time, TCA (Tennessee Code Annotated) 17-1-305 and TCA 17-117, together establish that, in general, the judge who presides over a case has control of the case for 30 days after the case is heard. However, if within that 30-day period, the subject of the case petitions for a new trial, and the presiding judge either dies or is removed from office because of insanity, then the petitioner automatically is granted a new trial. April 10, 1969 would have been thirty days after Battle heard Jimmy's case. Judge Preston Battle died on March 31, 1969, well before the April 10 deadline.

During this period, Nashville attorney Charles Galbreath was a judge with the Tennessee Court of Appeals. Like many lawyers and legal scholars throughout the country, Galbreath stated to the media, after Battle's passing, that Jimmy was guaranteed a trial by law – the statutes required it!

However, Jimmy never received the trial that the law guaranteed him. In fact, between those March 1969 petitions to Judge Battle and my brother's death on April 23, 1998, he and his defense team petitioned for a trial many times. He was turned down every time. Over the years, Judge Charles Galbreath has voiced his outrage, even writing to the U.S. Justice Department about this. Judge Galbreath has thoroughly researched the matter, and his findings are deeply troubling and they are worth reproducing in full:

It is too late to give James Earl Ray the trial he and most of the world wanted. To exhaust all reasonable efforts to find out if, and why, he 'Slew the Dreamer' alone or with one or more accomplices. As an appellate judge at the time of the second most publicized murder of this century my research into the legal problems surrounding his conviction on a plea of guilty raises a more perplexing issue than his guilt or innocence that has never been adequately dealt with. It is hoped that future research by historians will find the answer to why James Earl Ray was not granted a new trial.

The new trial was necessary to comply with the law. Being an enactment of the legislative branch of government neither the courts nor the executive branches had power to prevent it. But they both did by refusing to recognize and obey the law their members had sworn to uphold.

One of the dangers the law protects against is being illegally convicted. If, following conviction, it appears to the judge of the court irregularities or error occurred that lead to conviction the judge must grant a new trial. The law provides that only the trial judge may decide whether error has occurred on motion for a new trial. If for some reason the trial judge is unable to make that decision the law requires a ruling in favor of the defendant. If, for example, the court reporter should fail in a case to transcribe the testimony for review, a new trial must be granted on motion of the defendant. It used to be the opposite until the legislature provided for court reporters in all criminal courts and shifted the responsibility to the state to file the record. Thereafter, the defendant could not be penalized because state error had made it impossible for an appellate court to review what had happened at trial. So new trials followed as a matter of law if the record was not available.

All the foregoing legislative safeguards were enacted because judges refused to recognize and apply the needed protections by court rulings. The safeguards enacted by the lawmaking body of this state grants new trial for other reasons. One is when the death of the trial judge makes it impossible for him to correct errors that are alleged by a convicted defendant. It matters not if the errors are sustainable by proof. All that is required is that the error be described by the defendant and asked to be corrected in a timely manner followed by the death of the judge. This, of course, seldom happens. Tennessee Code Annotated 17-1-305 provides:

"When a vacancy in the office of trial judge exists by reason of death, permanent insanity as evidenced by adjudication, impeachment and conviction under article V of the Constitution of Tennessee, after verdict, but before the hearing of the motion for new trial, a new trial shall be granted to the losing party if the motion has been filed within the time required by rule of the court, and the motion is pending when the vacancy occurs."

Numerous cases following this code section show that in all cases in which it is applicable new trials had to be and were granted.

James Earl Ray filed a motion for a new trial contending his attorney, Percy Foreman, persuaded him to plead guilty against his will, telling him that was the only way to avoid death by electrocution. Coercion renders a plea invalid. Whether the claim of invalidity was true or not it stopped all proceedings in the case until a hearing could be held. Such a hearing never occurred because within a few hours after Judge Battle told his clerk to file the motion for a new trial he dropped dead. Under the law, that voided the plea by act of the general assembly.

Our Supreme Court ruled that James Earl Ray waived any right he had to a new trial by pleading guilty. Reason dictates that one may not waive error by challenging it. A much earlier Supreme Court in Tennessee, Swang v. State, 42 Tenn. 212 (1865), whose opinion was later dropped by the United States Supreme Court held, as have all courts since, that a plea of guilty may be challenged and voided by showing it was entered against the defendant's will.

It is an anomaly that it has been the judicial and executive branches of our government that have violated the law, not James Earl Ray. Although probably guilty he was never given his rights under the law to defend himself by the very entities supposed to uphold the law who denied his right to trial.

The rest is history. We await an answer to the reason James Earl Ray is the only person not granted this constitutional right under T.C.A.17-1-305" – Judge Charles Galbreath, Nashville, Tennessee.[1]

*** 

When I approach prosecutors with the fact that James Earl Ray, an accused assassin, was repeatedly and illegally denied a trial, they are always at a loss for words, simply speechless. In

---

1       Judge Charles Galbreath, letter to Mike Vinson and Jerry Ray, 1999.

fact, they appear to suffer from anxiety. Let me give you an example:

In November 1999, I traveled to Memphis to testify in the Loyd Jowers civil trial, the wrongful death lawsuit brought by Coretta Scott King and son, Dexter King against Jowers (see Chapter 4, the case of King v. Jowers and Other Unknown Co-Conspirators), charging him with a role in the slaying of Dr. King.

Loyd Jowers, at the time of Martin Luther King's assassination, owned and operated Jim's Grill, a café in Memphis, TN. Jim's Grill was located at 422 ½ South Main Street on the ground floor of Bessie Brewer's Boarding House (more commonly referred to as Bessie Brewer's Flophouse) where Jimmy had rented a room on April 4, 1968. The flophouse was near the Lorraine Motel where Rev. Dr. Martin Luther King, Jr. was assassinated. A jury found Loyd Jowers and other unknown co-conspirators guilty of the wrongful death of Dr. King.

Popular, long-time Memphis attorney Lewis Garrison represented Jowers. Attorney William Pepper represented the King family. (Pepper also served as lead defense counsel for Jimmy during the last fifteen years of his life.) After I took the stand that day at the Jowers trial, I went outside the Shelby County Court House and talked with a friend, wondering out loud why the Memphis District Attorney General's office, which has prosecutorial domain over the King assassination, was not participating in the Jowers civil trial. They declined an invitation to participate.

Just then, I noticed John Campbell of the Memphis District Attorney General's office walking up the sidewalk. For the last few years of Jimmy's life, Campbell was the main prosecutor over the King assassination. Campbell walked near us, ducking his head as if hoping he might sneak past us. I hollered out, "Hey, Big John Campbell!" He had no choice, so he stopped and said hello.

I quickly asked as many questions as possible: "Why aren't you participating in the Jowers civil trial? Why wasn't James Earl Ray granted a trial as guaranteed by Tennessee law?" For some reason, big John Campbell couldn't give a solid answer, and made it very apparent that he was in a big hurry to get away.

Campbell's behavior illustrates the cold disregard some judges and prosecutors exhibited toward my brother in his quest for a full-scale trial. As Judge Galbreath said in his excellent brief, " … it has been the judicial and executive branches of our government that have violated the law, not James Earl Ray."

*\*\**

After Jimmy's trial in Memphis, authorities transferred him to the state prison in Nashville, and once processed, they placed him in segregated confinement on Death Row. Naturally enough, this raised eyebrows, not just from his family, but also from all those on the outside looking in – legal professionals, the media, concerned citizens and in particular Jimmy and his defense counsel. My brother had received a 99-year sentence, not a death sentence.

At the time, Harry Avery was the Commissioner of Corrections for the State of Tennessee. Governor Buford Ellington appointed him to that position. In turn, Avery, in the role of lobbyist, had secured many votes for Ellington during his campaign. During Jimmy's first day at the state prison in Nashville, March 11, 1969, Commissioner Avery paid my brother a visit. Avery told Jimmy that he, Avery, was convinced that two St. Louis-based segregationists – real estate developer John Kaufman and Attorney John Sutherland – had hired Jimmy to pull the hit on King and had been paid $50,000.00 for doing it. Avery told Jimmy that he knew he had buried the money and Avery even offered to dig it up and place it in a bank for Jimmy's future. Avery went on explaining to Jimmy how he would be treated better if he cooperated with him concerning the supposed cash from the King hit and, also, if he would not appeal his conviction. Commissioner Avery assured Jimmy that he had clearance from the highest authority in making such an offer. Jimmy always figured the high authority was Tennessee Governor Buford Ellington.

Needless to say, since Jimmy had no such contract, no such payment, and no such 'hidden money' anywhere, this whole story from Avery was quite a stunning piece of fiction.

In addition to offering a 'helping hand' to Jimmy with his nonexistent loot, Avery also wanted to write a book about the King assassination. Every time I would drive to Nashville to visit Jimmy, Avery would make a point to greet me at the prison so he could talk to me. He let me know – in no uncertain terms – that if my brother would cooperate with him on the money and his book, things would be much easier for him during his stay at the state prison in Nashville.

Avery's pressure tactics went even further. Once, when Attorney Robert Hill went to the Nashville prison to confer with Jimmy, they discovered that Avery was listening in on them. Hill and Avery exchanged heated words over the eavesdropping, and news of their confrontation leaked to the press. Finally, not even Governor Ellington could cover for Avery and he was fired from his Commissioner's post in late May 1969. Avery's conduct toward Jimmy, and Avery's subsequent firing over the same, adds evidence to substantiate my allegations that Jimmy's case was repeatedly sabotaged and mishandled by relevant authorities from the time he was arrested and charged in the King assassination, until his death.

\*\*\*

Attorneys Stoner, Hill, and Ryan filed a motion some time in late 1969 to have Jimmy pulled off death row at the state prison in Nashville. Federal Judge William Miller heard the case in Nashville, Tennessee, several months after Jimmy's trial in Memphis. Only Hill and Ryan represented Jimmy; Stoner was on vacation in Germany. I was in the courtroom. Judge Miller ruled in Jimmy's favor – taking him off death row in Nashville. As a result of his ruling, in April 1970, Jimmy was transferred to Brushy Mountain state penitentiary outside Petros, TN. [In the Court of Appeals, Miller always ruled for Jimmy, while all the other judges ruled against him. Judge Miller was a compassionate man.]

As expected, most of the press was there that day to cover Jimmy's motion to get off Death Row. Also present was the famous author Gerold Frank who wrote *The Boston Strangler*, later made into a big-grossing movie of the same title, starring Tony Curtis, Henry Fonda and George Kennedy. Frank was planning to write a book about the King assassination and he talked to me that day. Frank eventually did write a book about the King assassination, titled *An American Death*, published in the early 1970s.

The thing that stands out most about Jimmy's hearing to get off death row was Judge Miller's request to review my brother's mental evaluation, which the prison psychologist was supposed to have conducted at the state prison. The psychologist took the stand and said he didn't have an evaluation because Jimmy had refused to talk to him. Judge Miller called Jimmy to the stand and asked if this was true. Jimmy said yes, it was and Judge Miller asked why he had refused to cooperate with the prison psychologist. Jimmy said, "I have enough problems as it is, without talking to shrinks. Besides, all they ever want to talk about is sex – did you ever desire to sleep with your mother, and all of that." The people in the courtroom burst out laughing. Judge Miller had to pound his gavel on his desk a couple times to restore order.

Also worth noting from that day was the conduct of Attorney Robert Hill. Whenever Judge Miller would rule in Jimmy's favor during the hearing, Hill, for some strange reason, would object, even though he was supposedly representing Jimmy. Attorney Richard Ryan just shook his head because he didn't agree with what Hill was doing.

However, thankfully, Judge Miller did rule in Jimmy's favor and he ordered the prison authorities to remove James Earl Ray from death row. After court, Gerold Frank came up to me and said, referring to Hill, "If that's the best your brother can do for a lawyer, he might as well give it up." Attorney Ryan, upset with the way Hill had conducted himself, said, "Jerry, I need a drink." After the hearing, Ryan and I walked to a liquor store in downtown Nashville where Ryan purchased a bottle of whiskey. As soon as we walked outside the liquor store, Ryan took a big, long gulp of it, sighed and said, "Man, I needed that!"

After Judge Miller made his ruling and the prison officials took Jimmy off death row and transferred him to Brushy Mountain State Prison, I returned to St. Louis and resumed helping my brother John in the Grapevine Tavern. Even though the Grapevine was showing a profit and John was paying me to help him, money wasn't coming in as much as I would have liked.

At the time, late 1969, I was living with an Italian woman named Rhonda. We shared an apartment in St. Louis. Since my salary from the Grapevine was not enough, Rhonda and I gave up our place in St. Louis and drove to Quincy, Illinois – my old stomping grounds, a hundred miles or so from St. Louis – to pick apples. Apple harvesting was in season. One day, while Rhonda and I were picking apples in a Quincy orchard, we were approached by two friends: John and Jim Rodgers. They told me they were planning to rob the Farmers Bank in Liberty, Illinois, about fifteen miles from Quincy. They wanted me to serve as the getaway driver.

I can't justify what I did over the next year or so, except to say that after all the experiences with crooked lawyers sabotaging my brother's defense, opportunistic journalists trying to make a buck off his situation, and every kind of government and law enforcement agency busy railroading my brother into prison for life, I was angry, really angry. I was angry and I was also broke. Maybe because I felt that I was under attack for no reason, trying to defend my brother Jimmy, I took up a life of crime again. I committed a series of armed robberies from which I netted several thousand dollars. I'm not proud of this, but I guess I acted in the only way that I knew to take out my rage and frustration against the world and also to bring in some badly needed money. Everybody had gotten rich off my brother, it seemed, and I was flat broke. The FBI records are available about all of this, if readers are interested.

After these robberies, and with the money I stole, I officially bought in with John as a partner in the Grapevine Tavern in St. Louis. John and I shut down the Grapevine for a week or so and used the robbery money to have it renovated. In fact, our partner in one of the bank robberies, was a good carpenter and he did the renovation work for us. We had a grand opening for the renovated Grapevine and had one hell of a turnout!

***

Attorney J.B. Stoner was still serving as Jimmy's lead defense counsel. As of February 1970, Stoner had declared that he was running against Jimmy Carter for Governor of Georgia. Stoner invited me to move down to his headquarters in Savannah, Georgia. He wanted me to work for him as security, helping with the campaign, etc. Since I was burnt out with the Grapevine Tavern and wanted to assist brother Jimmy in any way I could, I told John and Rhonda I'd catch 'em later, and headed for Savannah to work for Stoner.

Not long after I arrived at Stoner's Georgia headquarters in February 1970, Rhonda called to report that the FBI had quizzed her heavily about two of the bank robberies I'd committed, and she was worried. She said they even had talked to her mother. I told Rhonda, "Don't talk to 'em. And, when I say, don't talk to 'em, I mean not a single word. Ask 'em if they have a warrant. If they don't, shut the door." That's what Rhonda did, and the FBI finally stopped attempting to talk to Rhonda. Those were the last robbery that I ever committed. I hung up my mask and pistol after that. Even though the FBI did question me several times about other incidents, they never questioned me about the two robberies that Rhonda mentioned.

***

J.B. Stoner was one of the most blatantly outspoken racists of all time. He ran his Nazi-like N.S.R.P. organization from a small, though comfortable, complex in Savannah. The complex was a single-story building with about eight rooms, all under one roof. There was a main office where the secretaries and others worked. Stoner had his own private office. I slept in one of the extra rooms on a pullout couch.

In collaboration with Dr. Edward Fields, an officer in the N.S.R.P., Stoner published a right-wing magazine called *Thunderbolt*. J.B. was no stranger to the media and legal authorities. In the late fifties, he had been indicted for allegedly participating in the bombing of a black church in Alabama, but he had been acquitted. As noted earlier, J.B. was a huge fan of Adolph Hitler – his only criticism of Hitler being that he was "too moderate" in his treatment of the Jews. People in Georgia still talk about Stoner's television campaign ads in his race against Jimmy Carter. In his early forties at the time and wearing a dress suit and tie, Stoner would say, "This is Attorney J.B. Stoner, and I'm running for governor of Georgia. I don't want any Jew votes; I don't want any nigger votes; I only want white Christian votes. You can't have law and order and niggers, too."

The television stations didn't want to air J.B.'s campaign ads, but since he had paid for them, under campaign laws, they didn't have any choice. As soon as those ads would air, the telephones inside J.B.'s office would be ringing off the wall! We heard it all – threats, screaming, cussing, you name it – and understandably so.

Years later, after Stoner had moved N.S.R.P. headquarters to Marietta, Georgia, I vividly remember Byron De La Beckwith paying Stoner a visit. De La Beckwith had been accused of assassinating a black man named Medgar Evers, who was field secretary of the Mississippi NAACP, [National Association for the Advancement of Colored People] in front of Evers' Mississippi home in 1963. The courts tried him a couple of times in the sixties, but never convicted him. In the early nineties, De La Beckwith was retried, convicted and died in prison. There was a movie made about it. It's no wonder that Stoner and De La Beckwith were acquaintances – birds of a feather flock together.

Another person who hung around J.B. Stoner during his campaign for the governorship of Georgia was Don Black. Sometime in early summer 1970, Black came to Savannah on the pretense of campaigning for Stoner. At the time, Black was ... oh ... in his late teens, I'd say. He was an impressive young guy, big, tall, strong and intelligent. At that time, Black, even young as he was,

was the president of the American Nazi Party, an organization of the same ideology and intent as Stoner's N.S.R.P. Basically, they believed that the white race was far superior to all others. (I will respond to this question of racism and whether I am a racist and whether my brother James Earl is a racist, below.)

Even though Black was smooth and likable, I immediately sensed that he was up to something, and Stoner felt the same way. Black hung around the office at Stoner's N.S.R.P. headquarters for about a month. The problem, though, was that Black didn't do any campaign work for Stoner – handing out literature, going out and talking up Stoner – nothing. Instead, by just hanging around the office and talking to the secretaries and others who were trying to do the campaign work, Black proved to be disruptive.

One day, after he'd had enough, Stoner finally told Black he had to leave, that he didn't want Black hanging around the headquarters any longer. Black told Stoner that he was broke, had called his parents and they were wiring him some money to the office. Black had overheard J.B. ask me to go with him to a KKK rally to support Stoner's campaign, but told J.B. that I was suspicious of Black and that I was going to hang around the office to keep an eye on things. I didn't buy Black's story about being broke and money being wired to him. I figured it was merely a diversionary tactic to buy him more time around the office, with a specific objective in mind, even though I wasn't certain what that objective was.

After Stoner had left and it was almost dark, I was in the back office watching television and suddenly there was knock on the door! It was Don Black, obviously surprised to find me still at the office. Since it was common knowledge I accompanied J.B. practically everywhere he went – during that time fame, anyway – and Black had heard J.B. invite me to go with him to the KKK rally in Stone Mountain, Georgia, Black hadn't planned on me still being at the office. Black asked me if it was okay for him to hang around the office until his money arrived at the local Western Union Office. I told him to come on in, which he did.

At one point, the telephone in Stoner's office rang and I briefly went to answer it. When I came back from that call (a minute later), I caught Black coming out of the room where we kept the files containing the names and addresses of all the financial contributors to the N.S.R.P. Most contributors didn't want it known that they were associated with the N.S.R.P., and Stoner had agreed to keep their identities confidential.

I asked Black what was going on. He had a scared look on his face and said, "Something's come up, and I've got to go!" He ran out the front door. Immediately I went and checked the file room and, sure enough, all the cardboard boxes containing the individual files were missing. The window was raised and I looked outside. On the ground sat the boxes with the files. Now I knew what was up: Black planned to walk off with them.

I quickly ran into Stone's office, got a .38 pistol out of his desk drawer, and ran back into the file room. Not sure whether Black had any accomplices and not wanting to make myself an easy target for a possible sniper, I turned off the lights, moved toward the window, and waited. As Don Black came walking around the comer toward the boxes, I hollered, "Halt," but he kept walking. I hollered "Halt" again, but he kept walking toward me, reached down inside his belt, and pulled out a pistol. I raised my .38 and let off a round, hitting him in the chest. Not knowing how badly he was hurt, I ran around outside to him. The bullet had gone through his lung, and he was bleeding profusely, just about unconscious. I went back inside the office, and called the ambulance and the police. They were there in minutes. It turned out that the pistol I'd seen Black pull out was not a real one, but I had no way of knowing that at the time.

Don Black made it through the night and ultimately survived the shooting, for which I was grateful. However, the local D.A.'s office decided to prosecute me for attempted murder, and I had to make bail. Stoner made my bail. While I was out on bail and awaiting trial a few months later, it came on the news that my brother John had been arrested for being the getaway driver of a bank robbery in St. Peters, Missouri. All across the nation, the media started running stories about the "notorious Ray brothers" – one locked up for killing Martin Luther King, one about to go to trial for attempted murder, and one involved in a bank heist.

In November 1970, in Savannah, Georgia, I stood trial on the charge of attempted murder against Don Black; J.B. Stoner represented me. When Stoner called Black to the stand and questioned him, Black admitted that his sole purpose for coming to Savannah was to steal the files of the financial contributors to the N.S.R.P. so that he could recruit them to his American Nazi Party cause. The jury was out for only a few minutes before returning a verdict of not guilty. They concluded I had acted in self-defense. As Stoner later said, if it hadn't been for me being the brother of James Earl Ray, it never would have gone to trial to begin with, as obvious a case of self-defense as it was.

***

Over the years, many have attacked me for my association with Attorney J.B. Stoner and for attending an N.S.R.P. rally with him in Jacksonville, Florida, where he introduced me as the "Honorable Jerry Ray, brother of James Earl Ray." William Baxley, former Attorney General for the State of Alabama, had alleged that Jimmy, John and I knew Stoner before the King assassination, and that Stoner probably was in on it. Baxley had indicted Stoner in the late fifties over an alleged bombing. Baxley also had won a conviction against Robert "Dynamite Bob" Chambliss for the 1963 bombing of the Sixteenth Street Baptist Church in Birmingham, Alabama, a needless tragedy that left four young black girls dead.

Neither Jimmy, nor John nor I was aware that J.B. Stoner even existed until after the King assassination. The first time any of us had contact with him was shortly after the King assassination, when he came to Memphis and visited Jimmy in his jail cell and said he would represent him pro bono. So much for Baxley's crazy theory that the King assassination was a conspiracy involving the Ray brothers and racist attorney J.B. Stoner.

So, a good question is in order: if I'm not a racist, then why did I align myself with a racist like J.B. Stoner?

First, after the King assassination, with the media and the authorities out to get the Ray boys any way they could, I knew it would be difficult for me to hold a normal, everyday job. J.B. offered me a job and a place to stay.

Second, no matter what it took, no matter what was being said, I was desperate to help my brother Jimmy escape from prison, and I knew I could count on Stoner for help in planning and covering up those possible escapes.

Last, but not least, since stone cold Stoner was cool as a rock on ice, I knew that I could count on him to carry to his grave any confidences between us, come hell or high water. Yes, he was extreme right wing, but I knew he was not an informant. This benefited me. At that point, Stoner's racial perspective was irrelevant to me. However, my trust in his ability to keep his mouth shut was most relevant and I didn't want him talking about Jimmy's attempted escape.

That answers why I hooked up with the racist attorney J.B. Stoner.

Is Jerry Ray a racist? Is James Earl Ray a racist? The media has asked me these questions many times since 1968, but no matter what I say, they twist my words, trying to prove that Jimmy and I are racists. To me, it seems completely crazy that people even suggest this, but I've been accused of everything in the book. When I associated with J.B. Stoner, people assumed that if I associated with a racist like him, then I must be a racist too. When I associated and traveled with my friend Mark Lane, who is Jewish, they claimed I'm liberal.

I have many black friends – Dick Gregory, Martin Luther King's son Dexter King, and Judge Joe Brown. Again, I don't hate anybody or dislike anyone for their color, any more than I automatically like them because of their color. Nobody can help how he or she was born. Personally, no, I do not consider myself a racist.

The only people I don't like are people and politicians who cover things up. And all the people who cover things up in

Tennessee and in the government are white. In fact, everyone who prevented my brother from getting a trial and proving his innocence was white. Therefore, if I was a racist, I'd be more anti-white than anything! Over the years, black people and Jewish people offered the best support to Jimmy and me. We'd be crazy to be anti-something that supports us.

The one story that the media constantly twisted around to portray Jimmy as a racist was about the Leavenworth Honor Farm. They still use it against Jimmy to this day. Here's what really happened:

Between 1956 and 1959, Jimmy was doing time in Leavenworth Prison in Leavenworth, Kansas. As in many other prisons across the country, Leavenworth give prisoners who were close to being released an opportunity to transfer to an Honor Farm a few months before their release date. An Honor Farm was a special unit set up with relaxed rules and regulations to help the prisoners get used to being free, as it is hard to adjust to the outside after being locked up for so long.

When it came Jimmy's time, he refused to go. The reason being that he didn't want to risk the chance of getting into trouble when he was so close to being released. There was too much freedom at the Honor Farm. Visitors brought in drugs, etc., and other prisoners would try to set you up. He did not want to take a chance of getting arrested on drug charges because they take you back to court and give you more time.

The "official" story disseminated by the media insisted that Jimmy refused to go because the Honor Farm was racially integrated, and that he did not want to live among blacks. This accusation has always seemed crazy to me, as the general population at Leavenworth was also integrated, not just the Honor Farm. My friend, Dick Gregory, a black activist and comedian, said "It didn't make sense. The whole federal prison system is integrated!"

# CHAPTER SIX

# THE SNITCH &
# THE ESCAPE ARTIST

D uring April 1971, John had to stand trial for his alleged role as the getaway driver in the armed robbery of the Bank of St. Peters in St. Peters, Missouri. According to the police report, three men committed the robbery and supposedly John picked them up and drove them to their getaway spot.

As it happened, after King was killed and the FBI suspected that John and I had been involved in some bank robberies, the FBI sent a memo to all the relevant police and sheriff's departments that if any bank was robbed in their area, and if John Ray had recently been seen in the area, to arrest him as soon as possible – regardless of whether they had any evidence he was involved.

Of course, right after the robbery, the alarm went off, and the police were swarming all over the place. As bad luck would have it, John was nearby. His car had overheated, and the police spotted him stranded on the side of the road. Even though he was traveling alone, did not have in his possession a weapon or any loot from the St. Peters bank robbery, the police immediately arrested him as a suspect. The other three managed to get away, however, one fled to California and was eventually tried for a string of robberies in that state. The other two headed to Portland, Oregon where they were arrested for another incident and the police found some of the cash from the St. Peters robbery (approximately $50,000.00 total) on them.

Stoner agreed to represent John, so he and I traveled to St. Louis for the trial. Little did I know the FBI had been courting Catman Gawron in order to get him to testify against John. The FBI was paying Catman's bar tabs, keeping him tanked up on cheap wine, and playing on his ego, telling him what a good, smart guy he was – eventually persuading him to testify. Although he didn't come out and directly say that John was involved in the St. Peter's Bank robbery, he went on and on about how two of the robbers had hung out at the Grapevine and were big buddies with John.

Catman's testimony got John convicted of robbing the Bank of St. Peters, for which he was given a 20 year sentence at Leavenworth. The headline in the St. Louis Post-Dispatch, the main newspaper in St. Louis at the time, read, "Catman Turns Pigeon."

A few days after John was convicted, I picked up Catman Gawron, got him drunk and beat the shit out of him. When I had him about unconscious, I relieved him of what money he had in his wallet – a few hundred dollars. I continued driving and I kept thinking about his testimony against my brother John who hadn't done the robbery but got 20 years because of Catman's testimony. I don't know what it was, but I just saw red, and, once again, I started hitting Catman in the upper body and head with my fists and elbows. Then, my fury still on the rise, I slowed down the car, reached over, opened the passenger side door, and kicked Catman out of my car while it was still moving. When I put the pedal to the metal, he immediately let go, and I didn't care what happened to him.

After dumping Catman, I drove to my sister's house in St. Louis and spent the night. However, I hid my car way up the street at a friend's house. The next morning, the FBI came to my sister's house and said they wanted to talk to me. She told them that I wasn't there and she didn't know where I was. After the FBI left, she told me what had happened and I headed for Stoner's in Savannah, Georgia.

On my way to Savannah, I stopped off at a television station in Chattanooga, Tennessee. Being that I had been on television so much since the King assassination in 1968, the personnel at the station immediately recognized me as being James Earl Ray's brother and ushered me right on in. Back in those days, late sixties-early seventies, the name James Earl Ray was a hot topic and I could get on just about any show I wanted. It was a live interview – six o'clock news I'm pretty sure – and I gave the FBI and our justice system in general, pure hell! I went into detail about how the FBI had framed John.

The fact is, the FBI had absolutely no hard evidence on my brother John Ray concerning his alleged involvement in the St. Peters bank robbery. He was convicted on hearsay from other prisoners and he was given the twenty-year sentence solely because he was the brother of James Earl Ray – that was the deal! The System had to keep the public convinced that James Earl Ray was a racist thug who had murdered King in cold blood. Connecting his family to any felonious crime possible simply strengthened the System's stance. This is the manner in which authorities have handled the King assassination from day one – and continue to handle it!

Further, when John arrived at Leavenworth, Jim Rodgers, our friend who'd pulled some jobs with John and me, was already serving time there. Rodgers told John that the FBI had paid Rodgers a visit after John was arrested for the St. Peters job. The FBI told Rodgers that if he would implicate John in bank jobs we had pulled, the FBI would cut a deal with Rodgers and get him released early from Leavenworth. Rodgers told them where to go. My point again is that the FBI was not interested in solving bank robberies; rather, they were interested in ruining anyone in the immediate family of James Earl Ray, and they would stoop as low as necessary to do it.

Was my brother John involved in the St. Peters Bank robbery? I can't say for certain one way or the other. I didn't ask him, I wasn't involved, and I wasn't near the scene. The point is, John was convicted and served hard time on the flimsiest of hearsay evidence and without actual proof.

Last but not least, John Eugene "Catman" Gawron is the only man that I truly ever wanted to kill. It turned out that the snitch survived the beating I gave him and died a natural death.

***

After doing the television interview in Chattanooga, I drove straight to Stoner's headquarters in Savannah, Georgia. There was a letter from Jimmy waiting for me. On one of my visits to Brushy Mountain, Jimmy and I had set up an encrypted code that would let me know if he planned to escape! If, at the end of the letter, he signed off with "Jimmy" or "Jim," and placed two lines underneath his name, I knew that every seventh word in his letter would produce the message. Aside from the coded message, the rest of the letter didn't mean anything. After all of these years, I still have copies of these coded letters.

In addition to being security for Stoners' compound and for Stoner himself, I picked up mail for Stoner's N.R.S.P. at the Savannah Post Office. The first day I was back at Stoner's and had received Jimmy's letter, I delivered the mail to the Savannah Post Office and, as I came outside, two men in suits approached me and flashed badges. I knew, of course, they were FBI.

The FBI informed me they wanted to talk to me about Catman Gawron. I asked them if they had a warrant, and they said, no. I told them that was the end of our conversation, got into my car, drove off, and left them standing there. That was the only time I ever was questioned concerning Catman Gawron.

A few days later, I visited Jimmy at Brushy Mountain. My brother informed me that he was going to attempt an escape, needed some hacksaw blades, and wanted me to pick him up at a church that was located near Brushy Mountain. It was late April 1971, and the weather was starting to turn warm – more conducive to a successful escape than cold weather.

Returning to Savannah. I purchased the hacksaw blades and went to a shoe cobbler who placed the small hacksaw blades between the layers of my slip-on loafer soles. He compressed the layers and reattached the soles to my shoes.

About a week later, I drove back to Brushy Mountain Prison on visitation day and met with Jimmy, as always, in the big visiting room. The guard was there as usual, monitoring everyone. However, the guard was on the other side of the visitor's room. Luckily, Jimmy and I wore the exact same size shoe, size nine. So, while we were setting at the table and talking, we nonchalantly exchanged shoes underneath the table. After our visitation was over, I left and Jimmy went back into the prison population. Again, this was back in the days before the prisons had all these high-tech, sophisticated metal detectors, and that was how I was able to sneak the hacksaw blades to him the way I did.

Jimmy had instructed me to be waiting for him at 7 p.m. at a church near Brushy Mountain Prison grounds. Around 5:45 p.m., I loaded everything into my car. I had scored a .45 automatic pistol and a box of shells from Stoner, and I had taped them underneath my car so that, if I were stopped and searched, the police wouldn't find anything incriminating. I intended to give them to Jimmy once we got together. From there, our plan was that I would drive him to the nearest train station and he would go somewhere, let the heat die down a bit, then make another move. With the cash and pistol, he would have the means to survive and, hopefully, as he'd attempted to do before, get out of United States and start a new life somewhere else.

If this worked as planned, I had made up my mind that – more than likely – I never would see nor hear from Jimmy again. With him on the loose, I knew that the telephone lines at Stoner's and anyone else connected to the Ray family would be tapped, so Jimmy would never be able to safely call, regard-less of the country. Further, and more worrisome, there was a strong chance that he would go down shooting if the authori-ties caught up with him. And I knew he would be hunted the world over.

As planned, I arrived at the church near Brushy Mountain about at 6:45 p.m. with the .45 pistol and box of shells taped underneath the chassis of my car. I had been waiting about two hours when a car came up the road, pulled in behind me, and shined its lights. It was Brushy Mountain guards patrolling the area. I thought, Holy shit; we're screwed now. I wish I had the pistol where I could get to it!! Out of basic instinct more than anything else, I just sort of leaned over in the seat and acted as though I were asleep. I know it sounds hard to believe, but the prison guards just drove around me and proceeded to leave the area. To this day, I don't know what caused them to not check out my car.

As soon as the guards pulled away, I headed back to my hotel room in Harriman, Tennessee. I figured Jimmy's escape plan had not worked out. I turned on the radio, and it was all over the local news that James Earl Ray had been caught at-tempting to escape Brushy Mountain Prison. At the hotel, I turned on the TV and Jimmy's escape attempt was on all the major stations.

The next day I drove out to Brushy Mountain. The media was there, thick as ants on honey, and when I asked the warden to visit Jimmy, he turned me down. He said, "Jerry, you can't help him now." My brother later told me what had foiled his escape attempt.

Jimmy had planned this escape with a fellow prisoner called Jake "The Plumber" Morelock. As Jimmy tells in his book,[1] "Jake had access to pipe wrenches and other like stuff in his job as the jailhouse plumber, and Jake wasn't an infor-mant." Utilizing the wrenches Jake had scored and the hack-saw blades I had snuck to Jimmy, their plan, essentially, was to initiate their exit via a passageway located behind an ex-

1        Ray, *Tennessee Waltz*, 132.

haust fan. From there, they crawled to a manhole, which led to a tunnel housing steam pipes that led to "an opening in the wall to the outside"[2] After Jimmy made his way through this rather difficult maze, all he had to do was saw his way through a few bars that had been placed over the final opening leading to the outside. However, Jimmy and Jake did not figure a couple of factors into their escape formula.

First, when they tried to squeeze between the exhaust fan blades – which they'd bent with the pipe wrenches – Jake, a fairly large man, simply couldn't squeeze through. At that point, Jake made the decision to return to the cell. Jimmy, always slim and trim, was able to squeeze through, but when he reached the steam pipes, they were so damn hot, he had to back out, and before he knew it, the guards were all over him. Jimmy always thought that the guards had been alerted by the noise of Jake returning to their cell after not being able to squeeze through the bent exhaust fan blades. The warden stated that, due to the warm spring weather, the steam pipes would have been shut off on the first of May, and if Jimmy had waited until then to attempt his escape, more than likely, he would have been successful. If Jimmy had waited just a few days to attempt that particular escape, he might still be alive in some foreign country, and you might not be reading this book.

---

2        Ibid., 135.

Jerry Ray in front of Nashville State Prison in the late 1970s.
Photo courtesy of Jerry Ray.

# CHAPTER SEVEN

# LIFE AND DEATH
# IN PRISON

My brother never did manage to win his freedom, either legally through a trial or illegally by an escape. The closest Jimmy came was on June 10, 1977, when he and about five other prisoners successfully climbed over a wall at Brushy Mountain State Penitentiary in Petros, Tennessee, but they were recaptured three days later and returned to prison. Of course, I knew about this escape beforehand, as I had received a coded letter from Jimmy, dated May 17, 1977. Recently, an MSNBC television documentary called *Lockup: Inside Brushy Mountain*, featured my brother's famous escape. This escape attempt was Jimmy's final dance with freedom.

Because of this particular escape, and just by being the brother of James Earl Ray, I experienced some unique struggles and consequences. For instance, I was fired from my country club job after Jimmy's 1977 escape because I attracted news media and negative publicity from all over the place.

Another example is one of my favorite stories to tell and I've even told it on *Good Morning America*. A few days after my brother's attempted escape in June 1977, Geraldo Rivera, a popular talk show host, invited me to Boston – he even paid for my plane ticket – so I could appear on *Good Morning America* with him. I would be joined also by my friend and lawyer Mark Lane. Back then, I drove an old Cadillac and, on the way to

Chicago's O'Hare Airport to catch the flight to Boston for the *GMA* interview, that car just stopped dead – clunked out right on the road – and I couldn't get it started again. Well, guess what? The FBI was following in a car directly behind me, as they kept me under constant surveillance back in those days. They pulled up behind my stalled Cadillac, pushed it safely off the road, and gave me a ride to O'Hare. They even walked me right up to the airplane. At least the FBI is good for something!

Over the years, I didn't pay that much attention to what I went through because Jimmy is the one who really suffered. If I got fired, I didn't care – hell, I just got another job because I was a good, hard worker. Additionally, over the years, I've had to do things that I really didn't want to do, and got connected with people I didn't really agree with – like Stoner. However, I would do anything to help Jimmy's case.

Neither Jimmy nor I had ever heard of J.B. Stoner until after the assassination. When Jimmy was arrested in England, the press went wild with stories about him, and all of them assumed he was guilty. Jimmy wanted to fight these lies in the media and he heard that Stoner would represent him in this, for free. Jimmy already had a lawyer for the extradition and also for the murder charge – first Hanes and then Foreman. But after Foreman made him plead guilty, and Jimmy asked for a retrial and didn't get it, he fired Foreman and contacted Stoner for help. That's when he went before the judge who died, and Jerry filed an appeal of his previous conviction because of the forced guilty plea. Within a couple of years, Jimmy got rid of Stoner, but the press had made a big deal out of Stoner's racist, KKK, connections and that's why they assumed Jerry was racist. He wasn't. The only good thing about Stoner was that he was the kind of man who wouldn't betray a confidence and with all the bad press and railroading of Jimmy, he needed that. Later, I went to work for Stoner because I needed a job.

***

Jimmy's last year in prison was pure hell. He went in and out of a coma several times, and each time prison officials would rush Jimmy to the hospital, and later the hospital would return him to the prison. That cycle went on and on – back and forth – for about a year until he passed away. The reason Jimmy was so very sick was because of his liver. Previously, on June 4, 1981, several prisoners at Brushy Mountain Prison stabbed and sliced Jimmy with a twelve-inch shank in the prison library. A couple of days after the incident, I visited my brother at the hospital in nearby Oak Ridge, and I learned that he had twenty-two puncture wounds that required seventy-seven stitches, not to mention the slices all over him. While at the hospital, Jimmy received a blood transfusion tainted with hepatitis C, which eventually took a toll on his liver. After this stabbing incident, they transferred my brother to Tennessee State Prison – for his safety they claimed – where they kept him locked up for the remainder of his life. In 1997, when Jimmy became really, really sick, the transplant chief at the University of Pittsburgh Medical Center, Dr. John Fong, declared Jimmy eligible for a liver transplant. The Reverend James Lawson, a friend of Martin Luther King, who was with him when he was assassinated in 1968, raised money for the transplant through his Martin Luther King Truth and Justice Fund. Even Dr. King's family members supported the transplant drive. Sadly, but not surprisingly, a Tennessee judge ruled against it. He handed my brother a death sentence.

Thankfully, during his last painful year, Jimmy did not suffer in solitude. A man named Michael Gabriel became interested in my brother's case and moved from Baltimore, Maryland to Nashville, Tennessee. He would visit my brother each day and buy juice from the commissary to give to my brother. I would visit Jimmy twice a week.

It is bad enough to suffer like Jimmy did if he had committed the crime, but he suffered as an innocent man. It is really bad when you're in there innocent and you know you're innocent, and the politicians know you're innocent, and you still have to go through all of that.

My brother tried his best to get out when he was dying. Jimmy desperately wanted to die as a free man on the outside. We even had Tennessee government officials visit my residence, where I lived at the time.

They approved my living quarters and agreed that I could take care of my terminally ill brother in my home until he died. However, there was one condition to their dirty little deal – they wanted a deathbed confession of sorts. You know what they told Jimmy? They said, "We will let you out if you confess to the crime." I was there and Attorney William Pepper was there and we both witnessed this. They wanted my brother to confess to killing King, and if he did, they would release him and let him die outside of the prison. That's the only way they would let him loose. That's how low down and crooked those sons of bitches are! Well, Jimmy refused to confess to a crime that he did not commit, even for his own comfort, as sick as he was. Instead, he bravely faced what had become, in effect, a death sentence behind bars.

***

My brother passed away on Thursday, April 23, 1998, as a result of kidney failure and complications from liver disease. Jimmy was 70 years old.

Our family had Jimmy's remains cremated, and then placed his ashes in a nice blue and black ceramic urn. On Thursday, May 28, 1998, we held a memorial service for Jimmy at the Metropolitan Interdenominational Church on Eleventh Avenue, there in Nashville. In front of the church, we placed a picture of Jimmy beside his ashes. We decorated the church alter with pink and red flowers, and one red candle. I sat with my family in the front row of the church and prayed right beside Isaac Farris, a nephew of Martin Luther King, Jr. Before the service started, Rev. Edwin E. Sanders, pastor of this predominantly black congregation, who happens to be a black man himself, told our family, "We are happy and glad to open our doors to you."

Many people spoke at the memorial, including Rev. James Lawson, who had been a close friend of Martin Luther King, Jr. and a leader in the civil rights movement. He gave the eulogy. Rev. Lawson served as Jimmy's pastor after he was sent to prison, and he has thought for a long time that my brother was innocent. In his eulogy at the memorial he said, "James Earl Ray was not the assassin of Dr. King."

Coretta Scott King, Dr. King's widow, sent in a statement read by Isaac Ferris, a nephew of Martin Luther King, Jr:

> On this occasion we renew our determination for a full-scale investigation to seek the truth about the assassination of Martin Luther King, Jr. We were saddened by the physical pain and suffering James Earl Ray endured during the last months of his earthly life. We also shared … a deep regret at the tragic failure of the criminal justice system to give him his day in court, which is the birthright of every American.[1]

Unfortunately, Coretta and Dexter King [Dr. King's son] could not attend Jimmy's memorial because they had planned to be in Washington D.C. for an important meeting with President Bill Clinton about the existence of a conspiracy and to request a search for the truth.

To conclude the service, Dr. William Pepper, Jimmy's attorney until the day he died, gave the final speech at the memorial. He presented a much needed history lesson – for better than thirty minutes – on my brother's case, so the public and media could understand the injustice my brother endured. Pepper had worked many years trying to get my brother a trial, to prove that he did not kill King.

Over 200 people – white and black – attended the memorial service. Some said their final goodbyes to James Earl Ray, the alleged assassin of Reverend Dr. Martin Luther King, Jr. but I said goodbye to my brother, my brother Jimmy. I knew two

1        "Conspiracy Theory Kept Alive at Ray Memorial," *Chicago Tribune*, 29 May 1998,

things for sure: that I loved my brother and that he was an innocent man.

***

I thought Jimmy was innocent from the day he was picked
up until the day he died. After Foreman pleaded him guilty,
my brother fought from then until his death to prove his innocence. Unjustly, he never had a trial of his own, however; there
were two other trials that found Jimmy not guilty, including a
mock trial back in 1993 [April 4] on HBO, *The Trial of James
Earl Ray*, where the mock jury acquitted Jimmy, and the civil
trial in Memphis that I told you about earlier where Loyd Jowers testified. Both cases concluded: Ray not guilty of killing
King. That's why the courts would never let him go to trial.

Then, at long last, in 1997, due to new state laws in Tennessee, they reopened Jimmy's case. Attorney William Pepper
represented my brother, and he appeared before elected Memphis Judge Joe Brown. Judge Joe Brown got the case by rota-
tion. Ironically, the Judge happened to be a black man, and he
was also a weapons and ballistics expert. After reviewing the
evidence, he ordered new tests on the alleged murder weapon,
the Remington Gamemaster purchased by my brother.

The tests showed a heat mark on the bullets fired that did not
match markings on the bullet fragment, although that could
have been due to deposits in the barrel over time. In order to
complete the tests, Judge Brown requested copies of the earlier
FBI and HSCA [House Select Committee on Assassinations]
test results. The State Supreme Court in Tennessee stepped in
and denied him access because they said it went beyond the
parameters of the case on appeal. Judge Brown continued to
push for cleaning of the weapon and further testing, since the
testing was incomplete. Then, the Criminal Court of Appeals
removed Judge Joe Brown from the case. They accused him of
everything in the book – from bias on the bench to being on
a fact-finding mission. Judge Joe said to me personally, "The

State won't let the rifle be tested because they know it was not used in the assassination of King."

After Jimmy died on April 23, 1998, the case was closed, and the gun remained in custody of the Shelby County Courts in Memphis.

I continued to try to clear my brother's name, even after he had passed. I was certain he was innocent and I wanted to prove it for Jimmy's sake, and for the historical record. Several lawyers represented me pro bono, and they sued for repossession of my brother's gun. I figured, if I regained possession of Jimmy's rifle, we could get it cleaned and retested to see if it was the gun used in the assassination. Attorney and retired Judge Charles Galbreath filed a suit in 1999, then Attorney Bachrach – with the assistance of local council from Tennessee, Attorney Andrew N. Hall – filed a lawsuit in 2003. Judge Joe Brown, John Judge and T Carter also helped me in this last effort to have the gun tested. Not surprisingly, both times the Tennessee Courts denied me on the grounds that the rifle was "abandoned." In Tennessee, abandonment of property is defined as "the voluntary relinquishment there of by its owner with the intention of terminating his ownership, possession and control." [W.R. Grace & Co. v. Taylor, 55 Tenn. App. 2227, 398 S.W.2d 81 (1965)].

At some point, the [National] Civil Rights Museum, which now occupies the old Lorraine Hotel building where King stayed and was murdered, petitioned the Shelby County Court to donate the rifle and some other of my brother's possessions for historical exhibition at the Museum. In 2001, the Court agreed to transfer their control of the items to the Civil Rights Museum. After this announcement, Judge Brown and others increased their efforts to secure and retest the rifle before it broke the chain of custody, negotiating with both the Museum and Shelby County. (Judge Joe and Attorney Barry Bachrach even offered to pay for the testing with their own personal money.)

Without notice, under the cover of darkness, Shelby County transferred my brother's gun and other pieces of physical evidence to the Civil Rights Museum. They have it up on display there today. And, for a price, literally and figuratively, you can see it.

***

I wish someday somebody would try to get the gun out of the Civil Rights Museum and have it tested again. Every few years, experts invent new ways to test weapons and one of these new methods may prove beyond a doubt that the gun my brother purchased wasn't the gun used in the assassination. We will keep fighting for that. Like I said, I have always thought that my brother was innocent, and I believe the State of Tennessee and the U.S. Justice Department both know he is innocent. Otherwise, why would they rule against the law book and not give my brother a trial, and why do they fight so darn hard to keep from having the gun cleaned and retested? Well, I am a fighter too; I have fought against decades of injustice toward my brother.

I will continue to fight as long as I am alive.

AT THIS SITE
WILL BE ERECTED

# THE DR. MARTIN LUTHER KING, JR.
# MEMORIAL

THE MEMORIAL WILL EMBODY THE MAN, THE MOVEMENT,
AND THE MESSAGE. IT WILL HONOR THIS 20TH CENTURY
VISIONARY WHO BROUGHT ABOUT CHANGE THROUGH THE
PRINCIPLES OF NONVIOLENCE AND EQUALITY FOR ALL.
IT WILL BE A MEMORIAL SYMBOLIZING PROMISE
AND HOPE FOR A BRIGHTER FUTURE FOR HUMANITY

ALPHA PHI ALPHA FRATERNITY, INC.
IS THE SPONSOR OF THIS MEMORIAL

DEDICATED BY:

ADRIAN L. WALLACE
GENERAL PRESIDENT
ALPHA PHI ALPHA FRATERNITY, INC.

JOHN H. CARTER
PROJECT MANAGER
THE WASHINGTON, D.C. MARTIN LUTHER KING, JR.
NATIONAL MEMORIAL PROJECT FOUNDATION, INC.

WILLIAM JEFFERSON CLINTON
PRESIDENT
UNITED STATES OF AMERICA

DECEMBER 4, 2000

# AFTERWORD

We study history to avoid repeating the mistakes of the past and to learn the lessons that the past reveals to us so that we might make a better tomorrow for ourselves. I think that the best way to express my appreciation of this book is to say that it is a timely reminder of something we tend to forget. Studying history does us no good if we are operating on the basis of erroneous assumptions of fact. With this book, we get the opportunity to hear the testimony of a type of witness that we seldom are exposed to. Mr. Ray's perspectives and accounts are certainly unexpected by the average person and perhaps shocking to some. Whether or not you lend credibility to his assertions and allegations, his story certainly provokes contemplation and you might profit from exposing yourself to it if only to reflect upon the basis for your incredulity.

I can see how some readers might be flabbergasted by some of the things that Mr. Ray experienced and by the choices he made. On the other hand, there is an old point of wisdom in the law that relates to an exception to the evidentiary rule against hearsay: the legal presumption is that it is highly unlikely that rational people voluntarily, and without compulsion, intentionally make false statements against their penal, pecuniary or personal interests. In other words, it is simply human nature that no sane person – even the kind who might otherwise readily lie for personal gain or advantage – is likely to intentionally make untrue statements that are clearly adverse to his own interests. If the speaker reasonably appears to be knowingly incriminating or defaming himself then it is reasonable to conclude that he is speaking the truth.

Two things stand out when I read this book. One is that Mr. Ray confesses to the commission of serious felonies that carry significant penitentiary time. While there may be issues related to statutes of limitation upon prosecution and evidentiary considerations that might immunize Mr. Ray from the practical consequences of his stipulated conduct, the candor with which he admits his actions does merit some degree of confidence in his veracity in light of the considerations mentioned above. The other is that a lot of what he contends is not implausible based on my rather intimate and personal knowledge of the facts in the case against his brother, the late James Earl Ray, convicted of the assignation of Dr. Martin Luther King, Jr.

While I have not been persuaded to adopt all of Jerry Ray's conclusions and deductions I must admit that the factual contentions upon which he appears to base his conclusions are certainly consistent with the circumstances and evidence in the case against his late brother for the murder of Dr. King. Most significantly, he alleges certain things that cause the occasional raising of the eyebrow for reasons that relate to having made a point supported by the circumstances of the case rather than incredulity. I also whole-heartedly agree with him that something is very wrong about this case, the case against his late brother. At the very least, the fact that I am firmly convinced – for a number of reasons – that the Remington 760 Gamemaster rifle in .30-06 caliber said to belong to the late James Earl Ray is not, in fact, the murder weapon is sufficient to gain my concurrence with his conclusions that something is greatly wrong.

Among other things, when the case of James Earl Ray was in front of me some fifteen years ago, it was readily apparent that certain persons whose duty it was to protect the public and uphold the laws of the land seemed peculiarly circumspect, as well as very uncomfortable with the prospect of vigorously pursuing the available and derivative evidence in this case. Most concerning was the fact that there was exculpatory evidence that was not pursued – and there was at least enough of it to establish 'reasonable doubt.'

I am particularly concerned with the aversion displayed by these factions relative to the imperative need to conduct a candid and vigorous investigation and the great issue that was taken with my determination to conduct a proceeding that, first and foremost, would not allow adversarial gamesmanship to deflect the proceedings from discovering facts and evidence. (My holding was that once the facts were ascertained, then adversarial tactics would be allowed in the course of determining the proper legal and just consequences of the developed evidence.) I note that the record as a whole strongly suggests that there was a deliberate suppression of both candor and evidence in the initial proceedings that first transpired four decades ago.

In particular, I remain very concerned with the reticence and resistance that was displayed toward conducting proper ballistics tests of the material in evidence, especially since the record of the early proceedings makes it clear that the first judge assigned to this case was also of the opinion that the ballistics tests were inadequate. Indeed, he ultimately entered a written order directing that the rifle be retested. Considering the gravity of this particular case, it seemed otherwise logical at the time to presume that there would be an overwhelming determination to perfect the historical record and to at least conduct adequate ballistics tests using modern scientific methodology that had not been available in 1968. That there was such fierce resistance was shocking, especially as the ballistic material in the case was never subjected to a competent and adequate test regimen in the initial proceedings. The atmosphere was heavy with the cloying stench of aversion; there seemed to be a profound apprehension that some sort of governmental impropriety would be disclosed. This reflected the same climate prevailing at the end of the sixties that produced the Watergate imbroglio and fiasco. Watergate likewise had revealed the improprieties unlawfully committed by out of control officials and agencies who failed to comprehend that their actions threatened to subvert the fundamental underpinnings of the republic.

Moving on from this particular matter, we might note in our pursuit of an understanding of our past and our history that as the past recedes into deeper time, we become separated from the passions that colored the perceptions of those who were personally involved in the surrounding circumstances, and in the unique events that arose at the time and created that historic moment. As the student is removed from the immediacy of the events that he is studying by the inevitable passage of time and/or as he finds himself distanced from the immediacy of any personal experience that he may have had with the events he studies, the more likely he is to be dispassionate and objective in his analysis of those events. Objectivity is served even better if the events that are the focus of the student occurred outside of his or her lifetime.

But just what are those events that he seeks to analyze and understand? What really happened? Though the passage of time perhaps leads to and promotes some degree of dispassionate objectivity in analysis, it also has a downside for the simple reason that at some point, those witnesses with an actual living memory of the targeted events will have dimmed memories even if – as is inevitable – they have not all passed away. It is also inevitable, however, that some will have left their accounts for posterity. Not everyone leaves a written account of their doings in life and for those who do – as far as history is concerned – it is as though they almost literally wrote the account in stone. The select few who write such accounts plant the equivalent of fossils that future researchers will have to dig up and analyze. These writers tend to be closely affiliated with those who were actually present and participated in the significant historical moments – if not actually being the prime actors, as is often the case. They are representative of the people whose actions, determination and exercise of will often dictated the immediate as well as the ultimate outcome of the events that drove the affairs of the day. One common observation that reflects this is that what becomes accepted as history is most likely to be what is said of it by those who prevailed, those who 'won the day.' In contrast, the voice of the vanquished often becomes muffled and lost in the fog of the past without achieving much obvious impact on the future.

It is significant that you will get a chance to read the recollections and opinions of Mr. Ray. It is exceptional that someone in his circumstances is willing and able to bequeath his living memory to the historical record. For better or worse, you will be exposed to a side of things and an account that is not ordinarily recorded. Entertain yourself by reading his story and do yourself a favor by taking it as an opportunity to be expansive in your reflections about your own circumstances. Life can be exciting and it can be dangerous. At the bottom of it all, please reflect on the ultimate nexus in all of this and know that freedom and liberty do not come easily or safely. It is a dangerous thing to be free; it is even more dangerous to stand up for it and speak out on its behalf.

Is the lone outcast the dangerous entity? Is such an entity even present here? Or is the larger entity – the system that is supposedly designed to protect and serve us – the real danger if we depend upon it to obviate and replace the need for our personal involvement in the zealous maintenance of the "Land of the Free and the Home of the Brave?"

Judge Joe Brown

March 2009

# PHOTOGRAPHS

Above: Jerry Ray in the early 1980s.
Below: Jerry Ray in front of the Grapevine Tavern, St. Louis, Missouri.
Photos courtesy of Jerry Ray.

Above: Jerry Ray talking with Dan Rather in 1977. Mr. Rather had just Interviewed James Earl Ray.
Below: Geraldo Rivera interviewing James Earl Ray in the early 1990s.

Photos courtesy of Jerry Ray.

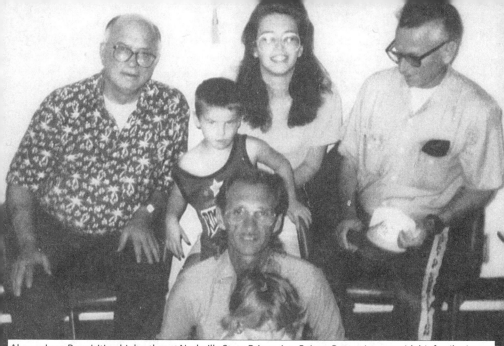

Above: Jerry Ray visiting his brother at Nashville State Prison. L to R: Jerry Ray; an inmate with his family; James Earl Ray. A prison photographer took the picture in 1997, four months before James slipped into a coma.
Below: James Earl Ray standing in the prison yard, Nashville State Prison Special Needs Unit a few months before he died in 1998. His damaged liver caused his stomach to retain fluid and swell.

Photos courtesy of Jerry Ray.

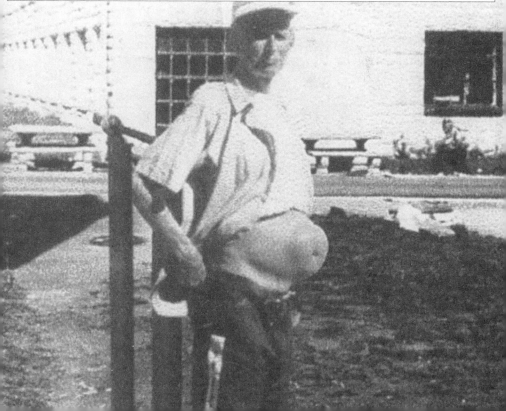

Above: L to R: Mike Vinson, Jerry Ray, Marty Bragg, Tamara Carter, Judge Joe Brown and Ken Holmes at a history conference in Dallas, TX.
Below: Jerry Ray, Tamara Carter and Judge Joe Brown clowning around at the Paramount Hotel, Dallas, TX, 1997.

Photos courtesy of Tamara Carter.

Above: Jerry Ray telling a story at Campise's Egyptian Lounge and Restaurant in Dallas, TX, 1997.
Photo courtesy of Jerry Ray;
Below: A coded letter written by James Earl Ray to his younger brother Jerry Ray on May 17, 1977 just before James Earl Ray's attempt to escape from Brushy Mountain Prison on June 10, 1977.
Courtesy of Jerry Ray and Michael Gabriel.

May 17, 1977

Dear Jerry:

Since you did not show up I assume you had car trouble I thought maybe you should have got rid of the cadillac long ago and got another smaller car. If I went any place I would like to be able to depend on the car or else bury it in the junk yard. All articles you sent me arrived alright, came by next day. Do you remember which highway you came down on, did you come by Jack's hotel ?

If you would have come back sunday we could have gotten everything straightened out including the writs. However, as you mentioned you can probably fly down and take care of everything in a ½ day. Most of the difficult legal work is over and there is not mush travling to do as I thought there would be.

take it easy.

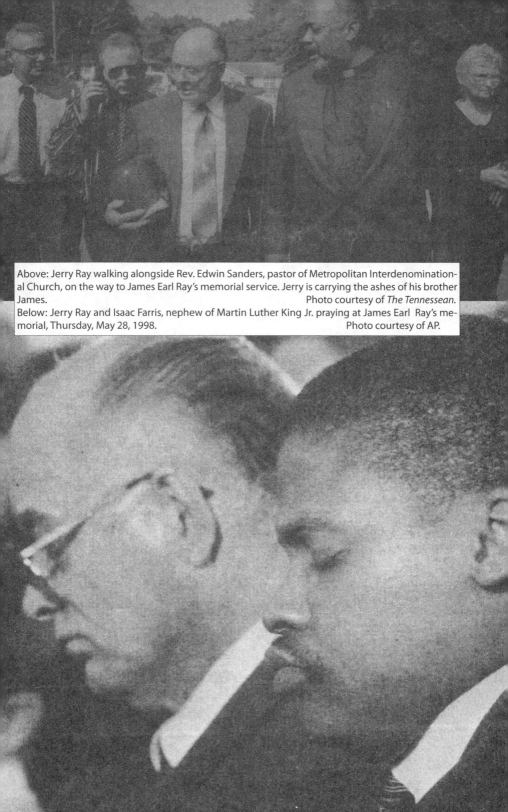

Above: Jerry Ray walking alongside Rev. Edwin Sanders, pastor of Metropolitan Interdenominational Church, on the way to James Earl Ray's memorial service. Jerry is carrying the ashes of his brother James.                                   Photo courtesy of *The Tennessean*.

Below: Jerry Ray and Isaac Farris, nephew of Martin Luther King Jr. praying at James Earl Ray's memorial, Thursday, May 28, 1998.                                   Photo courtesy of AP.

# BIBLIOGRAPHY

## Government Documents

Federal Bureau of Investigations. *Jerry Ray Files*. Washington, D.C., 91-35511, 91-34552, 91-Meredosia.

Federal Bureau of Investigations. *Jerry Ray Files*. St. Louis, Missouri, 91-38065, 91-5279, 91-5094, 91-Meredosia.

Federal Bureau of Investigations. *Jerry Ray Files*. Springfield, Illinois, 91-4774, 91-4653, 44-561.

Federal Bureau of Investigations. *Jerry Ray Files*. Chicago, Illinois, 91-7145, 91-Meredosia.

## Executive Department Documents

United States Department of Justice. Civil Rights Division. *Donald Wilson Immunity Agreement*, by Barry F. Kowalski. Washington D.C., April 22, 1999.

United States Department of Justice. Civil Rights Division *United States Department of Justice Investigation of Recent Allegations Regarding the Assassination of Dr. Martin Luther King, Jr.* Washington D.C., June 2000.

## Legislative Documents

United States Congress. House. Martin Luther King, Jr. Records Collection Act of 2002: To provide for the expeditious disclosure of records relevant to the life and assassination of Reverend Doctor Martin Luther King, Jr. 107th Cong., second sess., H.R. 5762 (introduced 19 November 2002).

United States Congress. House. *Report of the Select Committee on Assassinations of the U.S. House of Representatives.* 95th Cong., 1979.

## Legal Documents

Trial Transcript, Martin Luther King, Jr. Assassination Conspiracy Trial. Case No. 97242-4 T.D. Circuit Court of Shelby County, Tennessee, Thirteenth District at Memphis. Coretta Scott King, Martin Luther King, III, Bernice King, Dexter Scott King and Yolanda King, Plaintiffs v. Loyd Jowers and other unknown co-conspirators, Defendants, November 15-December 8, 1999.

Law Suit, Civil Action No. 98P912, Return of James Earl Ray's Remington Gamemaster Rifle. Seventh Circuit Court for Davidson County, Tennessee Probate Division at Nashville. Jerry Ray, Executor of the Estate of James Earl Ray, Plaintiff v. State of Tennessee, Defendant, June 1999.

Law Suit, Return of James Earl Ray's Remington Gamemaster Rifle. Criminal Court of Tennessee for Shelby County at Memphis. Jerry Ray, Executor of the Estate of James Earl Ray, Plaintiff v. William Gibbons, District Attorney General of Shelby County, Tennessee, William Key, Criminal Court Clerk of Shelby County, Tennessee and State of Tennessee, Defendants, March 2003 and October 2003.

## Newspapers

*Belleville (Illinois) News-Democrat,* February 14, 1997.

*Chattanooga Times Free Press,* April 8, 2001.

*Chicago Daily News,* 1968.

*Chicago Sun Times,* 1968.

*Chicago Tribune,* May 29, 1998.

*New York Times,* April 5, 1968.

*St. Louis Post-Dispatch,* April 1971.

*Southern Standard, (McMinnville, Tennessee),* April 24, 1998.

*The (Nashville) Tennessean,* 1968, 1997-1999.

## Books

Armstrong, John. *Harvey & Lee: How the CIA Framed Oswald.* Arlington, Texas: Quasar, 2003.

Blair, Clay Jr. *The Strange Case of James Earl Ray.* New York: Bantam Books,1969.

DiEugenio, James and Lisa Pease, ed., *The Assassinations: Probe Magazine on JFK, MLK, RFK, and Malcolm X.* Port Townsend, Washington: Feral House Publishers, 2003.

Frank, Gerold. *An American Death: The True Story of the Assassination of Dr. Martin Luther King.* Garden City, New York: Doubleday, 1972.

Huie, William Bradford. *He Slew the Dreamer.* Montgomery, Alabama: Black Belt Press, 1997.

Lane, Mark and Dick Gregory. *Code Name "Zorro" The Murder of Martin Luther King, Jr.* Englewood Cliffs, New Jersey: Prentice-Hall, 1977.

McMillan, George. *The Making on an Assassin: The Life of James Earl Ray.* Boston: Little, Brown and Company, 1976.

Melanson, Philip. *Who Killed Martin Luther King?* Berkeley, California: Odonian Press, 1993.

Pepper, William F. *Orders to Kill: The Truth Behind the Murder of Martin Luther King, Jr.* New York: Warner Books, 1995.

_____. *An Act of State: The Execution of Martin Luther King.* London and New York: Verso, 2003.

Posner, Gerald. *Killing the Dream: James Earl Ray and the Assassination of Martin Luther King, Jr.* New York: Random House, 1998.

Ray, James Earl. *Tennessee Waltz: The Making of a Political Prisoner.* Saint Andrews, Tennessee: Saint Andrew's Press, 1987.

_____. *Who Killed Martin Luther King?: The True Story by the Alleged Assassin.* Washington, D.C.: National Press Books, 1992.

Ray, John Larry and Lyndon Barsten. *Truth at Last, from the brother of James Earl Ray: The Untold Story Behind James Earl Ray and the Assassination of Martin Luther King, Jr.* Guilford, Connecticut: The Lyons Press, 2008.

Weisberg, Harold. *Martin Luther King: The Assassination (formerly titled Frame-Up).* New York: Carroll & Graf, 1993.

## Periodical Articles

"The Accused Killer RAY Alias GALT, the Revealing Story of a Mean Kid." *Life,* May 3, 1968, 20-29.

"The King Assassination Revisited." *Time,* January 26, 1976.

Cohen, Jeff and David S. Lifton. "A Man He Calls Raoul." *New Times,* April 1, 1977, 20-37.

Nieman, Robert. "Captain Jack Dean, United States Marshall, 20th Century

Shining Star." *The Texas Ranger Dispatch*, Winter 2003.

Vinson, Mike. "Jerry Ray Sounds Off." *Probe*, July-August, 2000, 33-34.

## Online Publications/Documents

Judge, John. "MLK Rifle Alert: Allow the Retesting of the Murder Weapon Alleged to have been the Murder Weapon in the Assassination of Martin Luther King, Jr." *CTKA/Probe*. http://www.ctka.net/alert-1.html (accessed 27 February 2009).

Maloney, J.J. "James Earl Ray." *Crime Magazine, an Encyclopedia of Crime*. http://www.crimemagazine.com/Assassinations/james.htm (accessed 9 February 2009).

_____."Who Shot Martin Luther King?" *Crime Magazine, an Encyclopedia of Crime*. http://www.crimemagazine.com/Assassinations/who.htm (accessed 11 February 2009).

Russell, Dick. "A King-Sized Conspiracy." *Dick Russell: Author and Environmental Journalist*. http:/www.dickrussell.org/articles/king.htm (accessed 10 February 2009).

# Index

# About the Author

**Tamara Carter** is an accomplished historian, researcher and archivist with expertise in the areas of political assassinations, social justice and Native American history. She holds a Master's degree in American History from George Mason University in Fairfax, Virginia and a bachelor's degree from Minnesota State University, Mankato. Ms. Carter lives near Washington, D.C.

Since 1954, the world's most powerful people have met in secret once a year ... until now!

The True Story of

The Bilderberg Group

Daniel Estulin

3RD U.S. PRINTING — OVER 1,500,000 COPIES SOLD WORLDWIDE

# The True Story of the Bilderberg Group

BY DANIEL ESTULIN        NORTH AMERICAN UNION EDITION

**More than a center of influence, the Bilderberg Group is a shadow world government, hatching plans of domination at annual meetings ... and under a cone of media silence.**

THE TRUE STORY OF THE BILDERBERG GROUP goes inside the secret meetings and sheds light on why a group of politicians, businessmen, bankers and other mighty individuals formed the world's most powerful society. As Benjamin Disraeli, one of England's greatest Prime Ministers, noted, "The world is governed by very different personages from what is imagined by those who are not behind the scenes."

Included are unpublished and never-before-seen photographs and other documentation of meetings, as this riveting account exposes the past, present and future plans of the Bilderberg elite.

Softcover: **$24.95** (ISBN: 9780979988622 ) • 432 pages • Size: 6 x 9

## ShadowMasters

BY DANIEL ESTULIN

AN INTERNATIONAL NETWORK OF GOVERNMENTS AND SECRET-SERVICE AGENCIES WORKING TOGETHER WITH DRUG DEALERS AND TERRORISTS FOR MUTUAL BENEFIT AND PROFIT

THIS INVESTIGATION EXAMINES HOW behind-the-scenes collaboration between governments, intelligence services and drug traffickers has lined the pockets of big business and Western banks. Beginning with a last-minute request from ex-governor Jesse Ventura, the narrative winds between the author's own story of covering "deep politics" and the facts he has uncovered. The ongoing campaign against Victor Bout, the "Merchant of Death," is revealed as "move/countermove" in a game of geopolitics, set against the background of a crumbling Soviet Union, a nascent Russia, bizarre assassinations, wars and smuggling. DANIEL ESTULIN is an award-winning investigative journalist and author of *The True Story of the Bilderberg Group*.

Softcover: **$24.95** (ISBN: 9780979988615 ) • 432 pages • Size: 6 x 9

## Dr. Mary's Monkey

*How the Unsolved Murder of a Doctor, a Secret Laboratory in New Orleans and Cancer-Causing Monkey Viruses are Linked to Lee Harvey Oswald, the JFK Assassination and Emerging Global Epidemics*
BY EDWARD T. HASLAM, FOREWORD BY JIM MARRS

*Evidence of top-secret medical experiments and cover-ups of clinical blunders*
The 1964 murder of a nationally known cancer researcher sets the stage for this gripping exposé of medical professionals enmeshed in covert government operations over the course of three decades. Following a trail of police records, FBI files, cancer statistics, and medical journals, this revealing book presents evidence of a web of medical secret-keeping that began with the handling of evidence in the JFK assassination and continued apace, sweeping doctors into cover-ups of cancer outbreaks, contaminated polio vaccine, the genesis of the AIDS virus, and biological weapon research using infected monkeys.

Softcover: **$19.95** (ISBN: 0977795306 ) • 320 pages • Size: 5 1/2 x 8 1/2

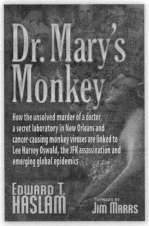

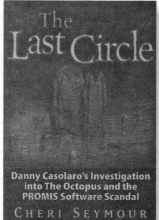

## The Last Circle
### DANNY CASALARO'S INVESTIGATION INTO THE OCTOPUS AND THE PROMIS SOFTWARE SCANDAL
#### BYCHERI SEYMOUR

**Danny Casolaro's Investigation into The Octopus and the PROMIS Software Scandal**

CHERI SEYMOUR

*The Last Circle* is an unparalleled investigation into one of the most organized and complex criminal enterprises that American has ever seen.

Investigative reporter Cheri Seymour spent 18 years following the trail of the Octopus, probing the behind-the-scenes dynamics of a labyrinth that encompassed multiple covert operations involving a maze of politicians; NSC, CIA, and DOJ officials; organized crime figures; intelligence agents; arms sales; drug-trafficking; high-tech money laundering; and the death of Washington D.C. journalist Danny Casolaro.

Through law enforcement agencies as far-ranging as the FBI, U.S. Customs, police and sheriff's departments, and even the RCMP national security division, Seymour learned that the official head of the Octopus resided in the U.S. Department of Justice, supported by an out-of-control presidential administration, its tentacles comprised of a cabal of "Old Boy" cronies, true believers, who held that the end justified the means.

They gave corruption a new meaning as they stampeded through the Constitution, cowboyed the intelligence community, blazed new trails into drug cartels and organized crime, while simultaneously growing new tentacles that reached into every facet of criminal enterprise. The theft of high-tech software (PROMIS) for use in money-laundering and espionage; illegal drug and arms trafficking in Latin America; and exploitation of sovereign Indian nations were just a few of these enterprises.

*The Last Circle* educates and inspires because it proves that an average citizen can make a difference in exposing and bringing to justice high-level criminals. For readers who like mystery and intrigue, it is an interesting first-person account of a female sleuth's journey through the nation's most hidden criminal underworld.

Softcover • **$24.95** • ISBN 978-1936296002 •672 Pages

## America's Nazi Secret
### AN UNCENSORED HISTORY OF THE US JUSTICE DEPARTMENT'S OBSTRUCTION OF CONGRESSIONAL INVESTIGATIONS INTO AMERICANS WHO FUNDED HITLER, POSTWAR IMMIGRATION OF EASTERN EUROPEAN WAR CRIMINALS TO THE US, AND THE EVOLUTION OF THE ARAB NAZI MOVEMENT INTO MODERN MIDDLE EASTERN TERRORISTS
#### BY JOHN LOFTUS

Fully revised and expanded, this stirring account reveals how the U.S. government permitted the illegal entry of Nazis into North America in the years following World War II. This extraordinary investigation exposes the secret section of the State Department that began, starting in 1948 and unbeknownst to Congress and the public until recently, to hire members of the puppet wartime government of Byelorussia—a region of the Soviet Union occupied by Nazi Germany. A former Justice Department investigator uncovered this stunning story in the files of several government agencies, and it is now available with a chapter previously banned from release by authorities and a foreword and afterword with recently declassified materials.

John Loftus is a former U.S. government prosecutor, a former Army intelligence officer, and the author of numerous books, including *The Belarus Secret, The Secret War Against the Jews, Unholy Trinity: How the Vatican's Nazi Networks Betrayed Western Intelligence to the Soviets,* and *Unholy Trinity: The Vatican, the Nazis, and the Swiss Banks.* He has appeared regularly as a media commentator on ABC National Radio and Fox News. He lives in St. Petersburg, Florida.

Softcover •**$24.95** • ISBN 978-1-936296-04-0 • 336 Pages

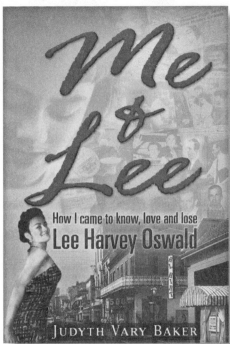

# Me & Lee

### How I Came to Know, Love and Lose Lee Harvey Oswald

**BY JUDYTH VARY BAKER**

**FOREWORD BY**

**EDWARD T. HASLAM**

JUDYTH VARY WAS ONCE A PROMISING science student who dreamed of finding a cure for cancer; this exposé is her account of how she strayed from a path of mainstream scholarship at the University of Florida to a life of espionage in New Orleans with Lee Harvey Oswald. In her narrative she offers extensive documentation on how she came to be a cancer expert at such a young age, the personalities who urged her to relocate to New Orleans, and what lead to her involvement in the development of a biological weapon that Oswald was to smuggle into Cuba to eliminate Fidel Castro. Details on what she knew of Kennedy's impending assassination, her conversations with Oswald as late as two days before the killing, and her belief that Oswald was a deep-cover intelligence agent who was framed for an assassination he was actually trying to prevent, are also revealed.

JUDYTH VARY BAKER is a teacher, and artist. Edward T. Haslam is the author of *Dr. Mary's Monkey*.

Hardcover • **$24.95** • ISBN 9780979988677 • 623 Pages

# PERFECTIBILISTS

### The 18th Century Bavarian Illuminati

**BY TERRY MELANSON**

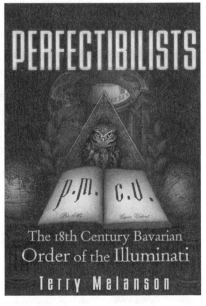

The shadowy Illuminati grace many pages of fiction as the sinister all-powerful group pulling the strings behind the scenes, but very little has been printed in English about the actual Enlightenment-era secret society, its activities, its members, and its legacy ... until now.

First choosing the name Perfectibilists, their enigmatic leader Adam Weishaupt soon thought that sounded too bizarre and changed it to the Order of the Illuminati.

Presenting an authoritative perspective, this definitive study chronicles the rise and fall of the fabled Illuminati, revealing their methods of infiltrating governments and education systems, and their blueprint for a successful cabal, which echoes directly forward through groups like the Order of Skull & Bones to our own era.

Featuring biographies of more than 400 confirmed members and copiously illustrated, this book brings light to a 200-year-old mystery.

Softcover: **$19.95** (ISBN: 9780977795381) • 530 pages • Size: 6 x 9

## THE 9/11 MYSTERY PLANE
### AND THE VANISHING OF AMERICA

**BY MARK GAFFNEY**

**FOREWORD BY**

**DR. DAVID RAY GRIFFIN**

Unlike other accounts of the historic attacks on 9/11, this discussion surveys the role of the world's most advanced military command and control plane, the E-4B, in the day's events and proposes that the horrific incidents were the work of a covert operation staged within elements of the U.S. military and the intelligence community. Presenting hard evidence, the account places the world's most advanced electronics platform circling over the White House at approximately the time of the Pentagon attack. The argument offers an analysis of the new evidence within the context of the events and shows that it is irreconcilable with the official 9/11 narrative.

Mark H. Gaffney is an environmentalist, a peace activist, a researcher, and the author of *Dimona, the Third Temple?*, and *Gnostic Secrets of the Naassenes*. He lives in Chiloquin, Oregon. Dr. David Ray Griffin is a professor emeritus at the Claremont School of Theology, and the author of *The 9/11 Commission Report: Omissions and Distortions*, and *The New Pearl Harbor*. He lives in Santa Barbara, California.

Softcover • **$19.95** • 9780979988608 • 336 Pages

## Rigorous Intuition
### What You Don'y Know, Can't Hurt Them
*BY JEFF WELLS*

"In Jeff's hands, tinfoil hats become crowns and helmets of the purest gold. I strongly suggest that you all pay attention to what he has to say." — Arthur Gilroy, Booman Tribune

A welcome source of analysis and commentary for those prepared to go deeper—and darker—than even most alternative media permit, this collection from one of the most popular conspiracy theory arguments on the internet will assist readers in clarifying their own arguments and recognizing disinformation. Tackling many of the most difficult subjects that define our time—including 9/11, the JonBenet Ramsey case, and "High Weirdness"—these studies, containing the best of the Rigorous Intuition blog as well as original content, make connections that both describe the current, alarming predicament and suggest a strategy for taking back the world. Following the maxim "What you don't know can't hurt them," this assortment of essays and tools, including the updated and expanded "Coincidence Theorists' Guide to 9/11," guides the intellectually curious down further avenues of study and scrutiny and helps readers feel empowered rather than vulnerable.

Jeff Wells is the author of the novel *Anxious Gravity*. He lives in Toronto, Ontario.

Softcover • **$19.95** • 978-0-9777953-2-1 • 505 Pages

## The Octopus Conspiracy
### and Other Vignettes of the Counterculture
### from Hippies to High Times to Hip Hop and Beyond ...
*BY STEVEN HAGER*

*Insightful essays on the genesis of subcultures from new wave and yuppies to graffiti and rap.*

From the birth of hip-hop culture in the South Bronx to the influence of nightclubs in shaping the modern art world in New York, a generation of countercultural events and icons are brought to life in this personal account of the life and experiences of a former investigative reporter and editor of High Times. Evidence from cutting-edge conspiracy research including the real story behind the JFK assassination and the Franklin Savings and Loan cover-up is presented. Quirky personalities and compelling snapshots of life in the 1980s and 1990s emerge in this collection of vignettes from a landmark figure in journalism.

**STEVEN HAGER** is the author of *Adventures in Counterculture, Art After Midnight*, and *Hip Hop*. He is a former reporter for the New York Daily News and an editor of *High Times*.

Hardcover: **$19.95** (ISBN 0975290614) • 320 pages • Size: 6 x 9

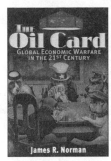

# The Oil Card
### Global Economic Warfare in the 21st Century
BY JAMES NORMAN

**Challenging the conventional wisdom surrounding high oil prices, this compelling argument sheds an entirely new light on free-market industry fundamentals.**
By deciphering past, present, and future geopolitical events, it makes the case that oil pricing and availability have a long history of being employed as economic weapons by the United States. Despite ample world supplies and reserves, high prices are now being used to try to rein in China—a reverse of the low-price strategy used in the 1980s to deprive the Soviets of hard currency. Far from conspiracy theory, the debate notes how the U.S. has previously used the oil majors, the Saudis, and market intervention to move markets—and shows how this is happening again.

James R. Norman

Softcover **$14.95** (ISBN 0977795390 ) • 288 PAGES

# Expendable Elite
### One Soldier's Journey into Covert Warfare
BY DANIEL MARVIN , FOREWORD BY MARTHA RAYE

A special operations perspective on the Viet Nam War and the truth about a White House concerned with popular opinion
This true story of a special forces officer in Viet Nam in the mid-1960s exposes the unique nature of the elite fighting force and how covert operations are developed and often masked to permit — and even sponsor — assassination, outright purposeful killing of innocents, illegal use of force, and bizarre methods in combat operations. *Expendable Elite* reveals the fear that these warriors share with no other military person: not fear of the enemy they have been trained to fight in battle, but fear of the wrath of the US government should they find themselves classified as "expendable." This book centers on the CIA mission to assassinate Cambodian Crown Prince Nordum Sihanouk, the author's unilateral aborting of the mission, the CIA's dispatch of an ARVN regiment to attack and destroy the camp and kill every person in it as retribution for defying the agency, and the dramatic rescue of eight American Green Berets and hundreds of South Viet Namese.

—NEW SPECIAL VICTORY EDITION— Commemorating our Free Speech Federal Court triumph that allows you to read this book exposing the true ways of war!

—READ THE BOOK,"THEY" DON'T WANT YOU TO!—

**DANIEL MARVIN** is a retired Lieutenant Colonel in the US Army Special Forces and former Green Beret.
Softcover: **$19.95** (ISBN 0977795314) • 420 pages • 150+ photos & maps

# Fighting For G.O.D.
### (Gold, Oil, Drugs)
BY JEREMY BEGIN, ART BY LAUREEN SALK

**This racehorse tour of American history and current affairs scrutinizes key events transcending the commonly accepted liberal/conservative political ideologies — in a large-size comic-book format.**
This analysis delves into aspects of the larger framework into which 9/11 fits and scrutinizes the ancestry of the players who transcend commonly accepted liberal/conservative political ideologies. This comic-book format analysis examines the Neo Con agenda and its relationship to "The New World Order. This book discusses key issues confronting America's citizenry and steps the populace can take to not only halt but reverse the march towards totalitarianism.

Jeremy Begin is a long-time activist/organizer currently residing in California's Bay Area. Lauren Salk is an illustrator living in Boston.
Softcover: **$9.95**, (ISBN 0977795330) 64 Pages, 8.5 x 11

# Radical Peace
### BY WILLIAM HATHAWAY
### REFUSING WAR

THIS SYMPHONY OF VOICES — a loosely united network of war resisters, deserters, and peace activists in Afghanistan, Europe, Iraq, and North America — vividly recounts the actions they have personally taken to end war and create a peaceful society. Frustrated, angered, and even saddened by the juggernaut of aggression that creates more counter-violence at every turn, this assortment of contributors has moved beyond demonstrations and petitions into direct, often radical actions in defiance of the government's laws to impede its capacity to wage war. Among the stories cited are those of a European peace group that assisted a soldier in escaping from military detention and then deserting; a U.S.-educated Iraqi who now works in Iran developing cheaper and smaller heat-seeking missiles to shoot down U.S. aircraft after U.S. soldiers brutalized his family; a granny for peace who found young allies in her struggle against military recruiting; a seminary student who, having been roughed up by U.S. military at a peace demonstration, became a military chaplain and subverts from within; and a man who expresses his resistance through the destruction of government property — most often by burning military vehicles.

WILLIAM T. HATHAWAY is a political journalist and a former Special Forces soldier turned peace activist whose articles have appeared in more than 40 publications, including *Humanist*, the *Los Angeles Times*, *Midstream Magazine*, and *Synthesis/Regeneration*. He is an adjunct professor of American studies at the University of Oldenburg in Germany, and the author of *A World of Hurt*, *CD-Ring*, and *Summer Snow*.

Softcover: **$14.95** (ISBN: 9780979988691) •240 pages • Size: 5.5 x 8.5

## Fixing America
### Breaking the Stranglehold of Corporate Rule, Big Media, and the Religious Right
### BY JOHN BUCHANAN, FOREWORD BY JOHN MCCONNELL

*An explosive analysis of what ails the United States*

An award-winning investigative reporter provides a clear, honest diagnosis of corporate rule, big media, and the religious right in this damning analysis. Exposing the darker side of capitalism, this critique raises alarms about the security of democracy in today's society, including the rise of the corporate state, the insidious role of professional lobbyists, the emergence of religion and theocracy as a right-wing political tactic, the failure of the mass media, and the sinister presence of an Orwellian neo-fascism. Softcover: **$19.95**, (ISBN 0-975290681) 216 Pages, 5.5 x 8.5

## Fleshing Out Skull & Bones
### Investigations into America's Most Powerful Secret Society
### EDITED BY KRIS MILLEGAN

"From original 19th-century rosters and nearly forgotten archives right up to recent aerial photos of the Bonesmen's 'Tomb,' no stone is left unturned in this must-read book for anyone desiring to know the truth behind this mysterious organization which has produced an unnatural number of national leaders. Names are named—including President George W. Bush—and the group's affiliation with a German Illuminati cell revealed, all in one well-documented volume." —Jim Marrs, journalist and author, *Rule by Secrecy* and *The War on Freedom*

This chronicle of espionage, drug smuggling, and elitism in Yale University's Skull & Bones society offers rare glimpses into this secret world with previously unpublished documents, photographs, and articles that delve into issues such as racism, financial ties to the Nazi party, and illegal corporate dealings. Contributors include Anthony Sutton, author of America's Secret Establishment; Dr. Ralph Bunch, professor emeritus of political science at Portland State University; Webster Griffin Tarpley and Anton Chaitkin, authors and historians. A complete list of members, including George Bush, George W. Bush, and John F. Kerry, and reprints of rare magazine articles are included.

Kris Millegan is the son of a CIA intelligence official. He has written articles for *High Times* and *Paranoia Magazine*. He lives in Oregon.

Softcover: **$24.95**, (ISBN 0-975290681) 216 Pages, 5.5 x 8.5

# The Franklin Scandal
### A Story of Powerbrokers, Child Abuse & Betrayal
BY NICK BRYANT

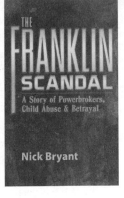

*A chilling exposé of corporate corruption and government cover-ups, this account of a nationwide child-trafficking and pedophilia ring tells a sordid tale of corruption in high places.* The scandal originally surfaced during an investigation into Omaha, Nebraska's failed Franklin Federal Credit Union and took the author beyond the Midwest and ultimately to Washington, DC. Implicating businessmen, senators, major media corporations, the CIA, and even the venerable Boys Town organization, this extensively researched report includes firsthand interviews with key witnesses and explores a controversy that has received scant media attention.

*The Franklin Scandal* is the story of a underground ring that pandered children to a cabal of the rich and powerful. The ring's pimps were a pair of Republican powerbrokers who used Boys Town as a pedophiliac reservoir, and had access to the highest levels of our government and connections to the CIA.

Nick Bryant is a journalist whose work largely focuses on the plight of disadvantaged children in the United States. His mainstream and investigative journalism has been featured in Gear, Playboy, The Reader, and on Salon.com. He is the coauthor of America's Children: Triumph of Tragedy. He lives in New York City.

Hardcover: **$24.95** (ISBN: 0977795357 ) • 480 pages • Size: 6 x 9

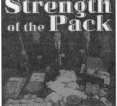

# Strength of the Pack
### The Personalities, Politics and Intrigues that Shaped the DEA
BY DOUG VALENTINE

*Through interviews with former narcotics agents, politicians, and bureaucrats, this exposé documents previously unknown aspects of the history of federal drug law enforcement from the formation of the Bureau of Narcotics and Dangerous Drugs and the creation of the Drug Enforcement Administration (DEA) up until the present day. Written in an easily accessible style, the narrative examines how successive administrations expanded federal drug law enforcement operations at home and abroad; investigates how the CIA comprised the war on drugs; analyzes the Reagan, Bush, and Clinton administrations' failed attempts to alter the DEA's course; and traces the agency's evolution into its final and current stage of "narco-terrorism."*

Douglas Valentine is a former private investigator and consultant and the author of *The Hotel Tacloban, The Phoenix Program, The Strength of the Wolf,* and *TDY.*

Hardcover: **$24.95** (ISBN: 9780979988653 ) Softcover **$19.95** (ISBN 9781936296095 ) • 480 pages • Size: 6 x 9

# A TERRIBLE MISTAKE
### THE MURDER OF FRANK OLSON AND THE CIA'S SECRET COLD WAR EXPERIMENTS
BY H.P. ALBARELLI JR.

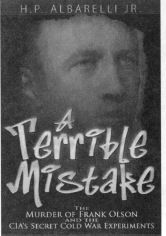

*In his nearly 10 years of research into the death of Dr. Frank Olson, writer and investigative journalist H.P. Albarelli Jr. gained unique and unprecedented access to many former CIA, FBI, and Federal Narcotics Bureau officials, including several who actually oversaw the CIA's mind- control programs from the 1950s to the early 1970s.*

*A Terrible Mistake* takes readers into a frequently bizarre and always frightening world, colored and dominated by Cold War concerns and fears. For the past 30 years the death of biochemist Frank Olson has ranked high on the nation's list of unsolved and perplexing mysteries. *A Terrible Mistake* solves the mystery and reveals in shocking detail the identities of Olson's murderers. The book also takes readers into the strange world of government mind-control programs and close collaboration with the Mafia.

H. P. Albarelli Jr. is an investigative journalist whose work has appeared in numerous publications and newspapers across the nation and is the author of the novel The Heap. He lives in Tampa, Florida.

Hardcover **$34.95** (ISBN 978-0977795376) • 852 pages • Size: 6 x 9
Softcover **$29.95** (ISBN 978-1936296088)

# The King of Nepal
## Life Before the Drug Wars
BY JOSEPH PIETRI

From the halcyon days of easily accessible drugs to years of government intervention and a surging black market, this tale chronicles a former drug smuggler's 50-year career in the drug trade, its evolution into a multibillion-dollar business, and the characters he met along the way. The journey begins with the infamous Hippie Hash trail that led from London and Amsterdam overland to Nepal where, prior to the early 1970s, hashish was legal and smoked freely; marijuana and opium were sold openly in Hindu temples in India and much of Asia; and cannabis was widely cultivated for use in food, medicine, and cloth. In documenting the stark contrasts of the ensuing years, the narrative examines the impact of the financial incentives awarded by international institutions such as the U.S. government to outlaw the cultivation of cannabis in Nepal and Afghanistan and to make hashish and opium illegal in Turkey—the demise of the U.S. "good old boy" dope network, the eruption of a violent criminal society, and the birth of a global black market for hard drugs—as well as the schemes smugglers employed to get around customs agents and various regulations.

Softcoverr • **$19.95** • 9780979988660 • 240 Pages

# Cannabis and the SOMA Solution
BY CHRIS BENNETT

*FROM KENEF PRESS*

"Scholarly, hip, witty, and extremely well documented . . . this book might cause a revolution in biblical studies!" —Robert Anton Wilson, author, Schrodinger's Cat Trilogy

"This book is fascinating! There can be little doubt about a role for cannabis in Judaic religion ... there is no way that so important a plant as a fiber source for textiles and nutritive oils and one so easy to grow would have gone unnoticed, and the mere harvesting of it would have induced an entheogenic reaction." —Carp P. Ruck, professor, Boston University

Seeking to identify the plant origins of the early sacramental beverages Soma and Haoma, this study draws a connection between the psychoactive properties of these drinks and the widespread use of cannabis among Indo-Europeans during this time. Exploring the role of these libations as inspiration for the Indian Rig Veda and the Persian Avestan texts, this examination discusses the spread of cannabis use across Europe and Asia, the origins of the Soma and Haoma cults, and the shamanic origins of modern religion.

Chris Bennett is an expert in the use of ethnobotanicals. He has contributed articles to numerous magazines, including *Cannabis Culture* and *High Times*, and he is the author of several books, including *Green Gold the Tree of Life: Marijuana in Magic and Religion and Sex, Drugs, Violence and the Bible*. He lives in British Columbia

Softcover • **$24.95** • 9780984185801 • 661 Pages

# The Hunt for Kuhn Sa
## DRUG LORD OF THE GOLDEN TRIANGLE
### BY RON FELDER

FOR TWO DECADES, the Burmese warlord Khun Sa controlled nearly 70 percent of the world's heroin supply, yet there has been little written about the legend the U.S. State Department branded the "most evil man in the world"—until now. Through exhaustive investigative journalism, this examination of one of the world's major drug lords from the 1970s to the 1990s goes behind the scenes into the lives of the DEA specialists assigned the seemingly impossible task of capturing or killing him. Known as Group 41, these men would fight for years in order to stop a man who, in fact, had the CIA to thank for his rise to power. Featuring interviews with DEA, CIA, Mafia, and Asian gang members, this meticulously researched and well-documented investigation reaches far beyond the expected and delves into the thrilling and shocking world of the CIA-backed heroin trade.

Ron Felber is the CEO of Chemetell, North America, and the author of eight books, including *Il Dottore: The Double Life of a Mafia Doctor, Presidential Lessons in Leadership*, and *Searchers: A True Story of Alien Abduction*. He lives in New Jersey.

Softover • **$19.95** • ISBN 9781936296156 • 240 Pages

# Mary's Mosaic
## MARY PINCHOT MEYER & JOHN F. KENNEDY AND THEIR VISION FOR WORLD PEACE
### BY PETER JANNEY
### FOREWORD BY DICK RUSSELL

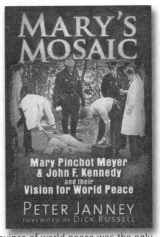

CHALLENGING THE CONVENTIONAL WISDOM surrounding the murder of Mary Pinchot Meyer, this exposé offers new information and evidence that individuals within the upper echelons of the CIA were not only involved in the assassination of President John F. Kennedy, but her demise as well. Written by the son of a CIA lifer and a college classmate of Mary Pinchot Meyer, this insider's story examines how Mary used events and circumstances in her personal life to become an acolyte for world peace. The most famous convert to her philosophy was reportedly President John F. Kennedy, with whom she was said to have begun a serious love relationship in January 1962. Offering an insightful look into the era and its culture, the narrative sheds light on how in the wake of the Cuban Missile Crisis, she helped the president realize that a Cold War mentality was of no use and that the province of world peace was the only worthwhile calling. Details on her experiences with LSD, its influences on her and Kennedy's thinking, his attempts to negotiate a limited nuclear test ban treaty with Soviet Premier Nikita Khrushchev, and to find lasting peace with Fidel Castro are also included.

Peter Janney is a former psychologist and naturopathic healer and a cofounder of the American Mental Health Alliance. He was one of the first graduates of the MIT Sloan School of Management's Entrepreneurship Skills Transfer Program. He lives in Beverly, Massachusetts. Dick Russell is the author of *Black Genius: And the American Experience, Eye of the Whale, The Man Who Knew Too Much*, and *Striper Wars: An American Fish Story*. He is a former staff writer for *TV Guide* magazine, a staff reporter for *Sports Illustrated*, and has contributed numerous articles to publications ranging from *Family Health* to the *Village Voice*. He lives in Boston, Massachusetts and Los Angeles.

Hardcover • **$29.95** • ISBN 978-1-936296-49-1 • 480 Pages

# America's Secret Establishment
## An Introduction to the Order of Skull & Bones
BY ANTONY C. SUTTON

**The book that first exposed the story behind America's most powerful secret society**

For 170 years they have met in secret. From out of their initiates come presidents, senators, judges, cabinet secretaries, and plenty of spooks. This intriguing behind-the-scenes look documents Yale's secretive society, the Order of the Skull and Bones, and its prominent members, numbering among them Tafts, Rockefellers, Pillsburys, and Bushes. Far from being a campus fraternity, the society is more concerned with the success of its members in the post-collegiate world.

Softcover: **$19.95** (ISBN 0972020748) 335 pages

# Sinister Forces
## A Grimoire of American Political Witchcraft
### Book One: The Nine
BY PETER LEVENDA, FOREWORD BY JIM HOUGAN

**A shocking alternative to the conventional views of American history.**
The roots of coincidence and conspiracy in American politics, crime, and culture are examined in this book, exposing new connections between religion, political conspiracy, and occultism. Readers are taken from ancient American civilization and the mysterious mound builder culture to the Salem witch trials, the birth of Mormonism during a ritual of ceremonial magic by Joseph Smith, Jr. and Operations Paperclip and Bluebird. Not a work of speculative history, this exposé is founded on primary source material and historical documents. Fascinating details are revealed, including the bizarre world of "wandering bishops" who appear throughout the Kennedy assassinations; a CIA mind control program run amok in the United States and Canada; a famous American spiritual leader who had ties to Lee Harvey Oswald in the weeks and months leading up to the assassination of President Kennedy; and the "Manson secret."

Hardcover: **$29.95** (ISBN 0975290622 ) • 396 pages • Size: 6 x 9

### Book Two: A Warm Gun
The roots of coincidence and conspiracy in American politics, crime, and culture are investigated in this analysis that exposes new connections between religion, political conspiracy, terrorism, and occultism. Readers are provided with strange parallels between supernatural forces such as shaminism, ritual magic, and cult practices, and contemporary interrogation techniques such as those used by the CIA under the general rubric of MK-ULTRA. Not a work of speculative history, this exposé is founded on primary source material and historical documents. Fascinating details on Nixon and the "Dark Tower," the Assassin cult and more recent Islamic terrorism, and the bizarre themes that run through American history from its discovery by Columbus to the political assassinations of the 1960s are revealed.

Hardcover: **$29.95** (ISBN 0975290630 ) • 392 pages • Size: 6 x 9

### Book Three: The Manson Secret
The Stanislavski Method as mind control and initiation. Filmmaker Kenneth Anger and Aleister Crowley, Marianne Faithfull, Anita Pallenberg, and the Rolling Stones. Filmmaker Donald Cammell (Performance) and his father, CJ Cammell (the first biographer of Aleister Crowley), and his suicide. Jane Fonda and Bluebird. The assassination of Marilyn Monroe. Fidel Castro's Hollywood career. Jim Morrison and witchcraft. David Lynch and spiritual transformation.The technology of sociopaths. How to create an assassin. The CIA, MK-ULTRA and programmed killers.

Softcover **$24.95** (ISBN 9780984185832 ) • 422 pages • Size: 6 x 9